BLACK ON WIGHT

THE STORY OF AN ISLAND'S NEWSPAPER

Isle of Wight County Press

BLACK ON WIGHT

THE STORY OF AN ISLAND'S NEWSPAPER

by Maurice Leppard

Published by The Isle of Wight County Press
Brannon House, 123 Pyle Street
Newport, Isle of Wight PO30 1ST

Designed and printed by Crossprint Design & Print
Daish Way, Dodnor Estate, Newport
Isle of Wight PO30 5XB

First published 2000
Copyright © The Isle of Wight County Press 2000

CONTENTS

INTRODUCTION

Every author knows those mixed emotions of anticipation and apprehension when they publish a new book – will it be a best-seller or remain on the shelf? In most cases the dilemma is quickly resolved and the author experiences elation or despair.

The budding weekly newspaper proprietor faces the same sort of situation but in his or her case those mixed emotions usually last a lot longer. Building up newspaper sales is invariably a gradual, capital-sapping business and so week in and week out the sales figures are pored over to see if the public is reacting favourably or not to the efforts of the paper's staff.

That, then, was the situation facing the two men who on November 29, 1884, launched the *Isle of Wight County Press*. The very title gave a clue to their boldness and ambition because it made clear that theirs was a paper for the whole Island – no mean challenge considering the logistics of serving a widely-spread population with distribution relying heavily and literally on horsepower.

Money may or may not be the root of all evil but it certainly bedevilled the association between the *County Press* founders, George Brannon and Edwin Fradd. As we will learn later, their partnership soon split up but fortunately a solicitor friend, Richard Roach Pittis, saved the day and within a year or two a group of local businessmen formed a company to run the *County Press* with George Brannon still very much a hands-on manager.

So the link forged between newspaper and Island in Queen Victoria's day survived and grew steadily stronger. Like any enduring relationship it was based on good faith and mutual respect – fundamental principles that are as vital as ever as the *County Press* and its readers enter the third millennium.

Not without good reason is the *County Press* often called the Island's Bible, as it has recorded over years, decades and now for well over a century the life and times of the Island with a near-religious zeal for accuracy.

The paper's vigour and creativity have been periodically renewed as personnel has changed, but, incredibly in an era of take-overs and mergers, a strong family connection remains with the Brannon family.

The value of that continuity at the helm of the *County Press* is incalculable. It has meant for example that employees have been treated with consideration and fairness, at a time when in many other companies they have become merely symbols on an accountant's software.

A clear indication of the worth of this family link was recognised in 1976 during a memorial service to Lt Col Wilfrid Brannon, son of the co-founder, George Brannon, who between them had overseen the paper's management for more than 90 years.

In a tribute to Col Brannon, Sir John Nicholson, the then Vice-Lord Lieutenant of the Island, said: "His best monument is his beloved newspaper. He was never its editor but it reflects in so many ways his adherence to certain principles of conduct, coupled with determination to reach the heart of a matter without fuss or ostentation and above all to serve the community."

The job of editing one of Britain's most successful and highly respected newspapers is rightly prized and there have been only seven editors in the 116-year history of the *County Press*.

Each has injected new ideas, some necessarily more than others. For most of the paper's history a guiding hand on the tiller, with only slight alterations in course, was all that was necessary; but in the last 30 years more radical navigation has been called for and meeting the challenge of competition has meant an updating of the layout and content.

Through all the changes the paper has jealously guarded its priceless reputation for integrity, for telling the truth without fear or favour. That is what successive generations of Islanders have come to expect. That is what they deserve. And that is what the *County Press* is pledged to continue to give them in the new millennium. ◆

ACKNOWLEDGEMENTS

On a personal note I want to place on record the invaluable help I have received in compiling this book from the chairman of the *County Press*, Richard Bradbeer, and his wife, Rosemary (nee Brannon), in sharing reminiscences of the family which is synonymous with the paper.

Mr Bradbeer showed tremendous foresight and insight in trawling through the minutes of meetings of the board of directors, making my task infinitely easier. I am also greatly indebted to the late Bob Lawn, junior, a former long-serving employee whom I have come to regard as the paper's unofficial historian, and to the compilers of the *County Press Golden Jubilee Supplement* of 1934 and the *Centenary Supplement* of 1984.

It is indicative of the close relationship between the paper and the Island that wherever I have turned for help it has been willingly given. An appeal for photographs to illustrate the earlier years of the *County Press* and the Island's history and make good a shortfall in our own archives met with a splendid response.

In this respect I would like especially to mention Roy Brinton, the Ryde historian and author, who generously allowed me to dip into his treasure trove of historic Island pictures, including a number taken by a late lamented mutual friend, Frank Taylor, of Carisbrooke.

My thanks also to Miss Susan Oatley, of the County Records Office; Mrs Fay Brown, of Ventnor and District Local History Society; author and journalist Adrian Searle, of Ryde; author and local historian Brian Greening, of Newport; Mrs Janice Cheverton, of Fishbourne; Roger Bartrum, of Wootton; Phil Bedding, of Cowes; Mrs Noreen Freeman and Mrs Mona Norman, of Newport; Mrs Phyllis Dukes, of Gurnard; Mrs Freda Snowdon, of Nettlestone; former Island councillor Ron Smith, of Totland; GKN Westland and Bembridge photographer Mrs Joy Warren.

I am indebted to Cowes historian Charlie Taylor for pointing me in the right direction in some of my external researches and to Ray Anker, a former *County Press* sub-editor, for his assiduous editing of this book. Last and by no means least my thanks to *County Press* chief photographer Chris Thwaites and past and present members of his team and to Cowes freelance photographer Ian Pert, a frequent contributor to the paper, for his special help in producing pictures for the book.

Maurice Leppard 2000

PREFACE

Keeping abreast of the times has been the paper's raison d'etre and what unimaginable changes – globally, nationally and locally – have taken place since it was first published, as mankind has leapt from the horse age to the space age.

There have been two wars that led to tremendous carnage and upheavals worldwide; the demise of the British Empire and, more recently, of Russia's Communist empire; incredible advances in science and medicine and significant social changes heralded by the emancipation of women and the onset of the welfare state.

Great manufacturing industries, like shipbuilding, have all but disappeared and so too have jobs for life in once such stable employment as banking, local government and farming.

The shrinking of the world in terms of travel, leading to the boom in foreign holidays, has been of great significance for a tourist area such as the Island.

When the *County Press* was launched the Island's economy depended heavily on farming for jobs and wealth creation. Mechanisation, with the tractor replacing the horse and the introduction of other labour-saving equipment and practices, led to a sharp reduction in agricultural employment. In more recent years farmers have been plagued by a series of problems, most notably the scourge of BSE mad cow disease. This brought sections of the industry to their knees and more recently a catastrophic drop in farmgate prices, controversy over genetically modified food and uncertainty over the equally emotive European Common Agricultural Policy, have thrown up new questionmarks for those who earn their living on the land.

Farming, however, remains one of the main planks of the Island's economy, as does tourism and manufacturing, which are facing problems linked to Britain's competitiveness.

The popularity of holidays abroad has resulted in many local hotels and guest houses being converted into homes for the elderly. The proliferation of these has marked another major change in the social fabric at large with the decline of the extended family concept of care.

Affected by rationalisation like many other industries, Island tourism has had to adapt to the end of the bucket and spade holiday era when families often spent a fortnight's holiday here. Now the average stay is less than a week, with short breaks the order of the day.

Undoubtedly an immense effort has gone into improving the standard of hotels, guest houses and holiday parks. Restaurants and pubs have adapted too, as eating out has become a regular social activity rather than a luxury. It is in this author's memory when the number of places to which one could go out for an evening meal on the Island could be counted on the fingers of one hand.

On the industrial front the Island can look back on a proud heritage of design creativity and craftsmanship of the highest order. The name of John Samuel White, of Cowes, will long linger as the builder of some of the finest destroyers, frigates and other ships.

At East Cowes, Saunders-Roe and its successor companies, now GKN Westland, have become a byword for versatility from record-breaking speedboats, through the massive Princess flying-boats, pioneering rocketry and the world's first hovercraft, to a position as a

Opposite **The staff of the *Isle of Wight County Press* at the beginning of the year 2000. Sitting (from left to right) are: advertising manager Alistair Porteous, production director Tony Thorpe, editor Brian Dennis, managing director Robin Freeman and company secretary George Harlow.**

global leader in the design and manufacture of composite components for airliners.

The Island has been placed in the forefront of radar technology at Somerton by Decca Radar, its successor Plessey Radar, through Siemens and now British Aerospace Defence Systems; and despite a chequered history that has seen several changes in ownership, Britten-Norman, of Bembridge, has made a major contribution to the Island's reputation for producing world-beaters with its versatile Islander aircraft.

Island companies have also shown themselves highly adept in advanced electronics and in providing software for the modern world's driving-force, computers. The growth of business parks to accommodate companies in this and other high-tech fields provides hope for the future. For example, Pascall Electronics, of Ryde, was awarded a £250,000 contract to build a control system for a satellite which will provide telecommunications for the United Arab Emirates.

In 1900 there were 20 motor vehicles on the Island. Today there are approaching 70,000, not taking account of the thousands of visiting cars and coaches in the summer, or the pantechnicons supplying the superstores that have taken such a heavy toll of the corner shop.

In terms of shopping, 1981 proved a watershed with the opening in February of the Island's first superstore, called Mainstop (now Somerfield), including a multi-storey car park above, in Pyle Street, Newport. July brought the arrival of Tesco's at Westridge, Ryde, the Island's first out of town superstore. More giants of the High Street were to follow.

The railways have experienced the reverse of what has happened on the roads, with the county's once all-encompassing steam rail network reduced to an electrified line service between Ryde Pierhead and Shanklin, operated by ex-London Underground stock. Fortunately the age of steam lives on, thanks to the IW Steam Railway at Havenstreet.

Cross-Solent communications have been transformed with the advent of the hovercraft, modern car ferries and catamaran passenger ferries, but, as we will find elsewhere in this book, the possibility of building a fixed link under or over the Solent resurfaces periodically and is a current controversial talking point.

In literature and the arts the *County Press* has witnessed great changes – from the days of Victoria's poet laureate Alfred, Lord Tennyson, at Farringford, through those of famous novelist and playwright J B Priestley, who lived on the Island for more than 20 years between the 1930s and 50s, to the Oscar award winning achievements of the Island's own native son, film director Anthony Minghella. And no-one who was around at the time will forget the massive pop festivals of 1969 and 1970.

With the world and the Island changing so much it goes without saying that the *County Press* has adapted to advances in newspaper processes at spectacular speed in the last decade.

While remaining faithful to its founding principles to report 'faithfully and boldly,' the presentation of the news, the greater use of photographs and colour and the big increase in the number of pages have kept it in tune with modern developments.

The introduction of computer-driven technology has had a massive impact on printers. Many have lost their jobs, mostly through early retirement, but others have retrained on computers, learning the new skills needed to create eye-catching advertisements on screen by following a mind-boggling list of instructions. Others play an important role on their computers as setters in-putting those copious readers' letters to the editor, along with hand-written or typed reports that have been submitted for publication.

When the author began his career with the paper almost 50 years ago those justly craft-proud descendants of Caxton were the lynchpins of production. The smell of molten lead is a lingering memory of the newsroom where linotype machines converted the red hot metal into slugs, as lines of type were known. Alongside them compositors deftly filled their galleys, inserting the characters upside down with a dexterity at which the layman could only marvel. In the foundry room too the acrid smell of hot metal pervaded as page plates were forged to slot on to the rotary press.

All these production procedures had in turn replaced earlier methods like those that existed when the first copies were printed with everything done by hand. Today the computer reigns supreme, feeding stories from the reporters' terminals, via the news editor, to the screens of the sub-editors, who check them for accuracy before making up pages on screen. After printouts have been made of the pages they come under the scrutiny of the editor and his deputy who mark up any corrections. These then return to the sub-editor responsible for the page to make the necessary amendments on screen.

A printout of the corrected page is passed to the media manager to process through the systems network to the output device, which picks up high quality images of pictures and advertisements before outputting the final page.

Since September, 1997, the *County Press* has been printed under contract by *The News* at its massive plant at Hilsea, Portsmouth. Although pages could be sent there electronically it has proved a rather costly and lengthy process. Ways of speeding this up are under investigation but for the time being page negatives are taken across to Hilsea for printing.

Having been so successful with the printed word, the *County Press* has made enormous strides in a short time in establishing a website rated as one of the finest of its kind in the country. The paper's website champion, Maurice Bower, has shown the sort of dedication evident when the paper itself was born.

Working closely with the New Media team at Hilsea, he started preparing for the site in June, 1998. It was functioning by the October and was launched officially the following January. Within three months the website earned widespread recognition when it was short-listed in a national competition sponsored by BT.

Net surfers can now find up-to-date news, sports, features, advertisements, an information desk and a tourist guide of the Island. Users of this new service are worldwide, many of them ex-Islanders delighted to be able to renew their acquaintance with the *County Press*. In November, 1999, for example, the number of page impressions, the most reliable measure of connections to a site on the worldwide web, topped 27,000. Visitors linking up to iwcp.co.uk were from around 40 countries, including the United States, Australia, New Zealand, Sweden, the Bahamas, France, Israel and even Mexico, Iceland and Azerbaijan.

Even so, 800 copies of the paper are still posted to mainland and international subscribers each week so that they too can keep in touch with the *County Press* and the Island. ◆

Isle of Wight County Press

AND SOUTH OF ENGLAND REPORTER

No. 1. NEWPORT, SATURDAY, NOVEMBER 29, 1884. [PUBLISHED EVERY FRIDAY NIGHT IN TIME FOR POST.] [PRICE—ONE PENNY.]

ADVERTISEMENT TARIFF.

The completeness and reliability of its local reports, the interest of its general contents, the care bestowed upon its production, and the arrangements made for its publication throughout the Isle of Wight, will combine to render the "County Press" the most valuable advertising medium in the Island. The charges for advertising are as follow:—

Official, Statutory, and Election Notices.— 6d. per line.

Trade Advertisements.—4d. per line. Contract ditto, 13 insertions, 2½d per inch. Special terms for running advertisements of half-column and upwards.

Small Prepaid Advertisements.—Servants Wanted and small "To Let" or "For Sale" advertisements, 20 words for one shilling, and fourpence for every additional eight words.

TERMS OF SUBSCRIPTION for the "County Press," delivered: By post—per quarter, 1/8; per half-year, 3/3; per year, 6/6. If paid in advance—per quarter, 1/6; per half-year, 3/-; per year, 6/-. Town subscribers—per quarter, 1/1; per half-year, 2 2; per year, 4/4. If paid in advance—per quarter, 1/-; per half-year, 2/-; per year, 4/-

CHAPTER ONE **IN AT THE BIRTH**

Spotting a gap in the market is how many successful businesses have started and the *County Press* is no exception. In the last quarter of the 19th century there were already a number of weekly papers published around the Island, including the *IW Times* at Ryde, the *Weekly Herald* (Cowes), the *Chronicle* (Sandown), the *Guardian* (Shanklin) and the *Mercury* (Ventnor), but there was no all-Island paper.

Contrary to previous accounts, the driving force in filling this gap was Edwin Fradd. He was born in South Africa where his father was a trader in Durban, but by the 1880s Edwin Fradd was married and living in Newport. Another sign of his intention to put down roots in the Island came when he took a commission in the IW Volunteers – a local version of the later Territorial Army battalions.

He needed a printer to turn his idea for a new paper into a reality and in 1884 formed a partnership with George Brannon. Mr Fradd was to invest £1,500, while for his part George Brannon would put in plant, machinery, expertise and goodwill, together valued at £1,000. An indication of the former's seniority in the partnership was that any profit would be divided two-thirds to him and one-third to Mr Brannon.

Premises were obtained on the south-east corner of Upper St James's Street and Pyle Street, Newport, later known as Tomlinson's Corner and now occupied by Abbey National.

The title *Isle of Wight County Press* not only reflected its all-Island coverage but also linked neatly with the growing campaign to separate the Island from Hampshire for local government purposes, which came to fruition with the first meeting of the IW County Council in February, 1890.

Thomas Lee, brother-in-law of Edwin Fradd, was appointed editor. He was an obvious choice because not only was he the respected local representative of the *Hampshire Independent*, the only newspaper widely circulated on the Island at the time, but had also edited a magazine called *The Island Quarterly*, containing the writings of a group of Islanders with a shared interest in literature.

The driving force behind the creation of the *Isle of Wight County Press*, Edwin Fradd

Opposite page **The very first issue of the *Isle of Wight County Press* which appeared on November 29 1884**

Left **George Brannon**

Centre **Thomas Lee**

Right **W H Dann**

As well as being the first professional journalist regularly working on the Island, Mr Lee was also a printer with premises in Pyle Street, Newport, not far from where the *County Press* first set up. He brought with him a contract for printing international seismological information which the *County Press*'s own jobbing printing department retained until several years after the Second World War.

The appointment as chief reporter of Mr W H Dann, BA, a Greek scholar among his other accomplishments, was in the longer run to prove an even more significant and farsighted decision than the recruitment of Mr Lee.

It was on November 29, 1884, that the first issue of the *Isle of Wight County Press* appeared, with a circulation of around 3,000. It was entirely set by hand, each individual letter and space assembled by compositors. The layout was based on *The Times* and since that style included a coat of arms at the head of the front page, it was decided the new paper would do the same.

The Knights Court Seal of the Island was chosen with a motto in the surrounding garter of Fideliter ac Fortiter - Faithfully and Boldly. The paper also billed itself as the *South of England Reporter*, an indication it would also carry mainland news, a move aimed no doubt at winning over readers from the *Hampshire Independent*.

The south-east corner of Upper St James's Street and Pyle Street was the first premises of the *Isle of Wight County Press*, now occupied by Abbey National

The existing printing staff of George Brannon was augmented by extra compositors and others were engaged to print the paper. Additional type, a quad-demy press and folding machines and power for driving them were obtained. Printing was done on flat sheets of newsprint, four pages at a time; then the paper was turned and another four pages were printed on the reverse. These were folded and cut, the whole process producing copies at the rate of about 1,000 an hour.

Those were the days when the printed word was still king, so it is not difficult to imagine the eagerness with which Islanders who could afford the one penny price bought that first issue. Advertisements had pride of place on the front page as they were to continue to do until 1974. Alongside Island and near-mainland news, the paper included reports of national and international events, as was the practice of many local papers.

In setting out their policy for the *County Press*, the proprietors emphasised their intention to publish an independent paper embracing the whole Island. Proceedings of local government bodies and all meetings of a public character would be fully and impartially reported by professional shorthand writers, backed up by a network of correspondents in every town and village – the forerunners of today's Village Talk correspondents.

"The attractions of our popular and rising watering-places and the beauty and salubrity of the Island generally will be kept prominently before the public," it was stated. "Agriculture, with the prosperity of which the welfare of the whole community is so closely linked, will receive special attention . . . and due space will be found for records relating to our great national sports and pastimes."

When the paper first appeared the Island had a population of about 75,000 and, as the editorial just quoted makes apparent, was heavily dependent on farming for generating wealth and employment. Newport itself was a garrison town, with hundreds of soldiers stationed in the area now occupied by Albany and Parkhurst prisons – many of them were responsible for injecting new blood into the Island as they married local girls.

Although reader-response to those early editions must have been encouraging there was a cloud hanging over the fledgling paper. Edwin Fradd's financial position was by no means as well-founded as his commitment to fund it appeared. He had several insurance policies in his own and his wife's name and was in the habit of borrowing against them.

While some reports have attributed his failure to sustain his arrangement with George Brannon to an inability to get money out of South Africa, the fact remains that the partnership was dissolved in July, 1885. Mr Fradd returned to South Africa, leaving his partner to carry on as best he could with the help of his solicitor and friend, Richard Roach Pittis.

While his own business acumen was perhaps not his greatest attribute, George Brannon showed determination and man-management skills that earned him great loyalty from his staff. Obviously the business was severely short of capital and a Newport accountant found the books "in great confusion and postings very much in arrear".

Mr Pittis saved the day by taking over Mr Fradd's share and responsibilities in the business and it was reconstructed as Brannon and Co, in the same month the original partnership ended. While George Brannon had to find extra capital himself, Mr Pittis considered that the paper had shown its value and ought to be maintained as an Island institution.

His confidence was rewarded and confirmation that the paper had in a short time become such an institution was underlined in April, 1886, when a complimentary banquet was given to editor Thomas Lee at the Bugle Hotel, Newport, presided over by Sir Richard Webster, QC, MP for the Island, supported by the mayors of Newport, Ryde and Yarmouth and other civic leaders.

The paper's high standing had other repercussions. People interested in sharing in its success began discussing the possibility of forming a company. Dr Milbourne Coombs and Mr George Long took a lead in this and, after consulting Mr W H Wooldridge, the Conservative Party agent for the Island, agreed to put the matter to the test.

There were plenty of takers and this led to the formation of the *Isle of Wight County Press* Newspaper and Printing and Publishing Company – second only in length on the register of companies to the Southampton, Isle of Wight and South of England Royal Mail Steampacket Company Limited (Red Funnel Ferries).

Five thousand £1 shares were offered and almost all were immediately taken up. In total 91 applications for shares were approved, varying from £2 to £300, with Philip Brannon, George Brannon's uncle, among the subscribers. The first recorded meeting of the board of directors, held at the Warburton Hotel (now Calvert's), Newport, was on April 6, 1887. Chairman was Col Archibald William Clarke and others present were Mr Pittis, Dr Coombs, Dr William Foster and Mr William Riddett.

George Brannon was not mentioned until his attendance at the second meeting the following month. It was then that the new company agreed to purchase the premises and plant from him and Mr Pittis for £4,000, paying a first instalment of £500. As part of the deal the two were allotted 1,750 fully paid up shares – 38.5 per cent of the issued capital – with 1,000 shares going to George Brannon and the remainder to Mr Pittis.

The new company's allegiance to the Conservative Party was specifically provided for in the Memorandum and Articles of Association. A council, a virtual shadow board of directors on which only the chairman of the board was eligible to sit, was set up to have the final say on political issues.

It was not unusual for newspapers to be directly aligned to a political party in this way and at one stage supporters of the Liberal Party acquired the *IW Express* published at Ventnor and plant for printing was set up in Newport. It ceased publication in 1903 and the copyright and title were acquired by the *County Press*. There were other challengers, the *Island Leader* (Jan 1906 to Nov 1909) and the *Island Star* (Nov 1910 to Dec 1919), printed and distributed by W Blake and Son, the Newport printers.

The *County Press*'s political council apparently met only once, but although there was never any question of which party the paper supported at elections, the editor usually received complimentary letters from all candidates after polling.

Things took an ugly turn, though, in December, 1910. The Liberal parliamentary

The Hoe Rotary Press installed in 1904

candidate, Mr Constantine Scaramanga-Ralli, circulated a leaflet implying that the company had been guilty of dishonesty. An action for libel was started but before the case came to court Mr Scaramanga-Ralli agreed to sign a letter of apology for publication and to pay the *County Press* £150 plus costs.

Some 60 years later the current chairman of the company, Mr Richard Bradbeer, launched a personal crusade to sever the political ties so that the paper could regain its original independence and this was achieved in the 1970s.

To return to those earlier years – the paper continued to flourish and by 1904 circulation had increased to 13,000. This was the year the board, now under the chairmanship of Mr Francis Templeman Mew, from a well-known Island brewing family, approved the purchase of a Hoe Rotary Press and new stereotyping equipment, which was installed at a cost of £1,100.

The rotary machine, powered by a Crossley gas engine and fed from a continuous reel of paper, was able to produce complete cut and folded papers at 8,000 to 9,000 an hour, compared to the time-consuming 1,000 copies an hour from the flatbed process.

No. 29 High Street, Newport, sold to the *County Press* in 1910

Thomas Lee, who had led the paper so successfully as editor since its inception, did not enjoy good health and retired in 1908. He continued, however, to write his popular Stylus notes for many years. Mr Lee died in 1921, aged 78. His successor, Mr Dann, had already proved his journalistic skills as chief reporter. A man of undoubted education, intellect and integrity, he was to fill the editorial chair until 1945, completing a remarkable 61 years with the *County Press*.

A classic anecdote of the days at the original premises, where the Brannon family lived over the shop, concerns an elderly gentleman living nearby who was known to be on his deathbed. As the midnight deadline for publication neared, a close watch was kept on his house and when all the curtains were drawn in the traditional sign of mourning the go-ahead was given for the obituary to be included in that week's paper. I am sure someone double-checked first . . .

The need for purpose-built premises was becoming pressing and when the directors heard that No. 29 High Street, Newport, was for sale for £2,200 they submitted an offer of £1,750 in May 1910. That month a deal was agreed with the owner, W W Kelleway, for £1,850. Known as the Tower House, the building suited admirably because it had land extending through to Pyle Street, which runs parallel to the High Street. Tower House had been formed from two Georgian houses with a Victorian facade, added apparently to blend with the Nash-designed Guildhall opposite.

Drawings and estimates for adapting the structure and adding a printing works at the Pyle Street end of the plot were accepted by the board. The architect, Mr J C Millgate, estimated the work would cost £2,000; in the event the lowest tender of £2,286, quoted by W H Brading and Son, was accepted. After building work was completed the transfer of the printing plant was obviously a formidable task and for the issue of Friday, September 13, 1912, the paper was printed by the *Evening News* at Portsmouth – an event that would have a significant sequel, as since September, 1997, the *County Press* has been printed by *The News* at Hilsea, Portsmouth.

Within two years of the *County Press* moving to its new home Britain was at war and the paper found itself in dire straits, not only through the absence on military service of key personnel but because of a chronic shortage of newsprint, aggravated by the inferior quality of what was available. One of the key men was the machinist, Robert Talbot Lawn. He was in the IW Rifles and until the regiment left the Island he was allowed by his CO to return to the *County Press* on Fridays to oversee the printing. When this handy arrangement ended, George Brannon himself took charge and ran the rotary press with the help of the assistant machinist.

This lasted until Sgt Lawn took his discharge from the Rifles on the expiration of his term when the regiment was in Egypt and he came back to the *County Press* in April, 1916. By the end of 1919 other members of staff had returned from the services, with the sad exception of Rifleman L. Hatcher, who was among the men of the IW Rifles who did not survive the epic battle at Suvla Bay in the disastrous Gallipoli campaign. The company erected a brass plaque to honour his memory

In July, 1917, the cover price of the paper had been raised for the first time, from one old penny to one-and-a-half-pennies, reflecting the increased costs arising from the war. Surprisingly, the price was again raised in March the following year to two pence, with the object of reducing demand in order to save on newsprint which was rationed to about one-third of the pre-war level. May, 1919, showed the board agreeing to raise the wage rate for printers by 12 shillings a week to £3, in line with a national agreement. The chief reporter, Mr Henry Allen, was on £3 10s. a week. The same year George Brannon's salary rose by £100 to £400 a year and Mr Dann had his salary increased by a similar amount to £350 a year.

George's son, Wilfrid, who had served with distinction in the war with the IW Rifles, was appointed assistant manager at £300 a year in February 1922. Two months later came another important appointment, that of Mr, later Sir, Henry Sweetman, JP, as chairman of the board. His other main business interest was in a brewery at Ryde. Those close to the company tell me that Sir Henry, for some unknown reason, was never very kindly disposed towards the Brannons, an attitude reflected in a rather niggardly approach to the salaries of both George and Wilfrid.

Having two years previously increased the share capital from £5,000 to £10,000 with a one for one bonus issue, the directors continued in buoyant mood. Their report to the annual

Lt Colonel Wilfrid Brannon in his ceremonial uniform as a deputy lieutenant

meeting in August, 1922, tendered their cordial congratulations to the shareholders "on the prosperous position of the company."

Just how tight a rein the board kept on affairs can be seen in November the following year, when George Brannon was instructed to obtain estimates for a wireless at head office. It cost £20, a lot of money in those days and an indication that the wireless system was still in its infancy.

In 1926 the usual good industrial relations at the *County Press* became entangled in the general strike in support of the miners. The paper's golden jubilee supplement of 1934 cryptically summed-up what happened: ". . . in obedience to the dictates of the TUC, union members of the *County Press* absented themselves from work. A day or two was, however, sufficient for them to realise the mistake their leaders had made".

November, 1927, saw the company purchase its first motor vehicle – an Austin 7 for the use of reporters who up to that time had to rely on public transport, motorcycles or cycles. The exception was the worthy chief reporter, Henry Allen, who had only one arm. He used a tricycle to visit outlying villages. Mr Allen's son, Gerald, followed in his footsteps on to the reporting staff and became chief reporter himself and later a sub-editor.

At the beginning of January, 1929, the share capital was doubled to £20,000 with another one for one bonus issue. July the next year saw the directors recommending dividends totalling 17 percent tax free. But despite the prosperity of the company it was not until November, after several months of discussion, that the directors agreed to raise George Brannon's salary to £1,000 a year, albeit backdated to the July. It may well have been that certain members of the board were envious of George Brannon's shareholding, because in May, 1932, they refused to transfer 670 shares from the will of Mrs Margaret White Popham to George's wife, Laura, and 130 to his daughter, Phoebe.

With circulation now topping 18,000, covetous eyes were being cast towards the prosperous *County Press* and in May, 1933, George Brannon told the board that an approach

The *County Press* staff and directors in the golden jubilee year of 1934

had been received from the *Daily Express*. He was instructed to reply that the paper was not on the market but that if the *Daily Express* was anxious to acquire it the directors "might be prepared to entertain a handsome offer for it". Whether the directors were serious or not about selling, the *Daily Express* apparently did not respond with a handsome offer.

In 1935 the board expressed congratulations to the chairman, Mr Sweetman, on his being knighted for public and political services in the Island. That year Capt H A Drudge, who was also the Island's Conservative Party agent, was appointed company secretary in succession to the late Mr G H Long, who had served the company faithfully since 1887.

More momentous changes were afoot. In October, 1936, the board approved the retirement of George Brannon, then aged 78, as managing director and agreed he could retain a consultancy and directorship on a rather miserly retirement pension, after 52 years devoted service, of £350 a year.

His son, Wilfrid, was appointed manager with no seat on the board and without any increase in his salary of £450. He officially took over his new responsibilities at the beginning of 1937, his father, the redoubtable co-founder of the company, handing over the reins as the old year passed away. George Brannon, without whom the *County Press*, would probably not have survived beyond infancy, died in 1938 and Wilfrid was appointed to fill the vacancy on the board.

An insider's epitaph for George Brannon came from Mr Bob Lawn, junior, who succeeded his own father as machine room foreman. "He was a great boss. Every morning when he came in at nine the first thing he did before opening the post was to come round and have a word with everyone, including the errand boy. He never barged in on anyone. He always let you know he was coming, so if you were smoking you could quickly put your cigarette out."

The minutes of the annual meeting of the board in August, 1938, which noted that Wilfrid Brannon had been appointed a Deputy Lieutenant of Hampshire and the IW, were the last recorded in manuscript in bound books. From then on they were typed on loose-leaf sheets.

The *County Press* having recently been accepted as a member of the Audited Bureau of Circulation, its certified sales in January, 1939, were recorded as 19,276 copies a week.

After just 21 years of peace Britain declared war on Germany on September 3, 1939, when Hitler's troops invaded Poland. It appeared that the management had stockpiled newsprint in anticipation of the outbreak of hostilities, because in December the same year the board noted there were about 320 reels in store – sufficient for about 65 weeks.

At the beginning of 1940 all employees in the works were placed on a 45-hour week, thus eliminating overtime pay! By March a further 45 reels of paper were received at £17 per ton compared with just over £11 per ton seven months earlier. By November 1940 newsprint had risen to £28 10s per ton.

With the Luftwaffe an ever-present threat, the *County Press* directors came to a reciprocal arrangement with the Portsmouth *Evening News* under which each would do the other's printing if it was halted by enemy action. Fortunately neither paper had to make use of this facility, although on April 7, 1943, the *County Press* front office was damaged when a bomb fell on the next door electricity shop, now a Southern Electric showroom.

In February the following year the by then Lt Col Wilfrid Brannon was welcomed back as manager in response to a plea from the directors that he be released from the army. Sir Henry Sweetman's 22-year tenure as chairman ended with his death on June 8, 1944, aged 86. He was succeeded by Mr E W Way, who held the position for five years before resigning on health grounds and being replaced by Mr H R Palmer, a prominent Island solicitor.

Mr Dann's 37 years in the editor's chair ended with his death in May, 1945. As previously noted, he had given the *County Press* a total of 61 years' service, successively and successfully as chief reporter and editor. He was succeeded by Mr Walter Sibbick, who had joined the paper as an office clerk in 1902 and was to hold the top editorial job for 15 years — the first and, at the time of writing, the only Island-born journalist to occupy the post.

Island born Walter Sibbick appointed editor in 1945

Being a shareholder in the company continued to be highly remunerative, as was shown in July, 1947, when the directors recommended a final dividend of ten percent, plus a bonus of 20 percent, making, with an interim of 20 percent, a total of 50 per cent for the year. The staff shared in the prosperity with a £700 bonus, which included £100 for the editor. Investment was not neglected and a Crabtree rotary printing press, costing £16,500, had its first live run in March, 1952, delivering 29,000 copies of a 12-page edition. The paper's talented cartoonist, Tom Smitch, whose creations had been such a popular feature for many years, suddenly found events taking a decidedly unfunny turn in April, 1953. According to the board minutes he submitted a cartoon not considered a fit subject by the editor, but which subsequently appeared in the *IW Times*. "Such action by an employee could not be entertained and Mr Smitch was given notice forthwith."

The board meeting of September, 1954, was notable for the presentation of a wireless set to Ernest Melhuish, newsroom foreman, in recognition of 60 years' sterling work. His father, Samuel, who died in 1920, was the first works foreman — another example of the firm's

The Crabtree Rotary press installed in 1952

remarkable tradition of family service. At the annual general meeting of the company a year later, a bonus issue of shares was agreed on a one for two held basis, increasing the capital from £20,000 to £30,000. In September, 1956, the current chairman of the board, Mr Richard Bradbeer, was appointed assistant works manager to Mr George Moth.

Two years later solocitor Lt Col William James Eldridge, one of the most senior members of the Island's law fraternity, was elected to the board.

He was to become the county's Vice-Lord Lieutenant and succeeded to the chairmanship of the board in January, 1976, following the death of Col Brannon.

Lt Col Eldridge held the position until his death in April, 1987, when he was succeeded by Mr Bradbeer.

Returning to the late 1950s, notice was received from the father of the chapel (works chairman) of the Typographical Association – the main printing union – of a work to rule from June 3, 1959. A national dispute had been rumbling for some time and the directors agreed to go along with the strategy of their own trade association, the Newspaper Society. This entailed giving all TA members two weeks' notice, coupled with an offer of re-employment on a day-to-day basis. An impasse was reached and the printers went on strike.

Richard Bradbeer (right) and George Moth (top centre) with other members of the foundry room team during the printing dispute of 1959

Here Mr Bradbeer takes up the story: "Led by Col Brannon setting type on an Intertype machine, a skeleton staff of management and apprentices turned to and for six weeks produced a 12-page paper. It was a very hot summer and George Moth, myself and one apprentice ran the foundry and the rotary press. It did wonders for the thirst and certainly the brewery came out a winner!"

In the middle of all this the board discussed the retirement of Col Brannon as manager and Mr Sibbick as editor. It was agreed the former's retirement would take effect from September 1, 1959, and that of the latter one year later. It was decided to offer Mr Moth the post of general manager, with promotion of Mr Bradbeer to works manager. But the changes did not end here. Mr Palmer announced his intention to resign as chairman and successfully proposed that Col Brannon should succeed him. Mr Palmer died in April, 1961, having been a director for 28 years.

Work returned to normal on August 6. The board was told that during the strike, publication of the paper had yielded an average weekly profit of £166, against a loss of £600 per week had production halted.

Mr Sibbick's long and loyal service with the company, including being on the board for 20 years, ended on a full-time basis on June 30, 1960. He continued as a consultant and to contribute his popular Vectensis notes, which he penned in an almost indecipherable scrawl.

In total Mr Sibbick was actively associated with the company for more than 75 years – an extraordinary achievement to which the author, who was appointed a junior reporter by him, is only too pleased to have the chance to pay tribute. He died, aged 89, in 1978.

His successor as editor was Mr Ernest Ash, a former editor of the *Worthing Gazette*, who had been the assistant editor of the *County Press* for eight years.

A few months later in 1960 another one for two bonus share distribution was made, raising the share capital from £30,000 to £45,000. Sales topped 30,000 for the first time in June, 1963, regarded as the paper's equivalent of breaking through the four-minute barrier for the mile and the directors sent a letter of congratulation to Mr Ash and his staff.

The death of Capt Drudge, company secretary since 1935 and a director since 1939, occurred in September, 1964. Ten years earlier he had been awarded the MBE for his political and many other services to the Island community. Capt Drudge, whose daughter, Mary, worked in the *County Press* front office before being comissioned in the Army herself, was something of a legend in his own lifetime having masterminded eight successive Tory parliamentary election victories on the Island.

He was succeeded at the *County Press* by Mr Cyril Blee, who, however, died in January, 1967, just a month after his 50th birthday. His successor was Mr Raymond Byerley, who held the post until retiring in September, 1980, when Mr Robert Crosbie took over. He in turn was succeeded in January, 1986, by the present company secretary, Mr George Harlow.

In May, 1966, Mr Moth, who had been pressing the issue for some time, must have taken great pleasure from a company pension scheme being launched. The continuing high profitability of the *County Press* was again reflected at the annual meeting in September, 1970. Dividends totalling 42.5 percent, less tax, were approved. That year, as a result of the introduction of decimalisation, the cover price of the paper was set at three new pence, an increase over the previous price of six old pence.

Mr Bradbeer became general manager in April, 1971, following the premature death of Mr Moth, who had been a highly respected executive of the company since becoming assistant works manager in 1948.

A 28-page edition was published for the first time in April, 1971. By February, 1973, circulation had reached 34,548. The *IW Times* at Ryde was bought for £3,000 in the same month from the investment company which had purchased the previous owners, Lightbowns. The move was undoubtedly a defensive measure by the company to prevent it being taken over by a possible rival. The *County Press* printed the *IW Times* for almost two years before closing it – a sad, if inevitable, end to a paper that had served Ryde and district well for 112 years.

The *IW Times*, incidentally, incorporated another Ryde paper, the *IW Observer*, which had started in 1845. For the record, there were other papers published in Ryde in the 19th century, including the improbably named *Earwig* and the *Ventilator*.

Mr Ash's near 13-year tenure as editor of the *County Press* ended in April, 1973, and he was succeeded by his assistant, Mr Stephen Rea, a bluff Lancastrian whose wide experience included working for the *Daily Mirror*.

Nationally a fourfold increase in oil prices proved a major threat to the economy, including

Above **Ernest Ash**
Below **Stephen Rea**

the possibility of newsprint having to be rationed. Its price rocketed to £107.56 per tonne, a 45 percent rise in ten months, but that was only the beginning of the newsprint crisis and within two years the price was £185.75 per tonne.

It was around this time that production facilities were coming under pressure again. The rotary press could print a 16-page paper but the *County Press* was now regularly running more than 16 pages and had to be printed in two sections – one on Thursday afternoon and the other on Friday, with the two sections inset one inside the other by hand.

Extra typesetting was achieved by increasing the number of Intertype machines and staff but the problem of printing and inserting was becoming more and more difficult. Thanks to the trade grapevine, Mr Bradbeer found the solution in an unlikely location – under the arches of Waterloo Station, or more accurately in a warehouse under the arches of that famous railway terminus. There, stored but beginning to get rusty, was a machine identical to the one owned by the *County Press*.

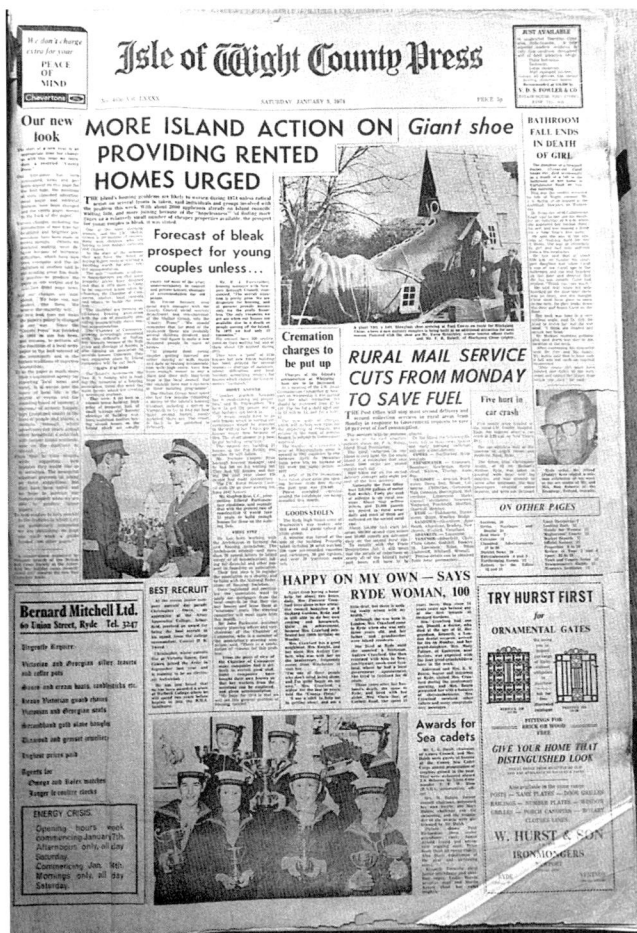

The first copy of the *County Press*, in January, 1974, to carry news on the front page

Mr Bradbeer explained: "I took the two units and tacked them onto ours. There was also an extra gadget that would print an eight-page section and rewind it back into a reel. Then, with the main printing run this preprinted section could be fed in at the same time to be cut and folded. It meant that we could now print a 32-page paper without inserting sections and when the pre-print was up and running, a 40-page paper was possible."

An extraordinary meeting of shareholders in September, 1973, changed the name of the company to the *Isle of Wight County Press Limited* and, more significantly, a new and revised Memorandum and Articles of Association were adopted under which the paper severed its links with the Conservative Party.

Despite all the problems caused by the escalation in fuel prices, senior management was not deflected from improving and updating the *County Press*. The layout was changed, spearheaded by news on the front page for the first time in January, 1974. The importance of this modernisation was to prove its worth because the paper was soon to face the most serious challenge in its history from a thrusting up-to-the-minute tabloid. Mr Rea, who was appointed a director in December, 1975, needed all his know-how in leading his editorial team against the rival.

The *IW Weekly Post* had been launched the previous month and after the original owners ran into serious financial difficulties it was taken over by Portsmouth and Sunderland Newspapers, which was able to put its formidable resources and expertise behind it. At one stage the *Post* was producing 80-page papers, brimful of news, features, sport and colour and claimed a readership in excess of 20,000. Incredibly, *County Press* circulation dipped only temporarily by a 1,000 or so, a clear indication that many Islanders were buying both papers each week.

At the beginning of 1981, in a response to the young rival's challenge, the *County Press* switched from its traditional Saturday publication to Friday – the same day as the *Post*. Significantly, the *Post* was never able to make any serious inroads into the *County Press*'s highly prized advertising from estate agents. In April, 1986, it was bought by newspaper entrepreneur Philip Davis, who in turn sold it in 1988 to a subsidiary of Middlesex County Press (Holdings) Ltd. Soon after that, circulation was split between paid-for copies in some Island areas, with free copies in others. Meanwhile, *County Press* sales were nearly 37,000 a week.

The *Post* finally ceased publication in November, 1990, after being converted to a free sheet, its owners blaming the closure on the economic climate and a recession, which, they said, appeared to be biting more deeply on the Island than elsewhere. Be that as it may, the *County Press* had seen off what at one time was a worthy challenger and whose presence had galvanised the paper into a much more go-getting approach, both editorially and in advertising and sales. The episode had proved that competition is healthy, if a little nerve-wracking at times . . .

An indication that the *Weekly Post* affair had not soured *County Press* relations with *The News* at Portsmouth came when the latter's presses were used to print the October 21, 1977, edition after a fire in the central panel of the rotary printing press at Newport.

When it came to introducing new technology the *County Press* directors adopted a canny wait-and-see policy, a strategy neatly summed up by Mr Bradbeer: "It is no part of a small weekly newspaper to be an innovator and experimenter. Leave it to the big boys, keep a beady eye on what is going on around you and when it looks right and all the bugs have been ironed out then that is the time to think seriously of spending money."

By 1975 some of the newspapers Mr Bradbeer and his colleagues were keeping an eye on were beginning to install phototypesetting. This was a method of typesetting on a computer. By using a simple keyboard, information was converted to punched tape, a strip of paper with a series of holes. The paper tape could then be read by a phototypesetting machine – literally producing a photograph of the typed story. Instead of the heavy, dirty process of making up pages in lead, it was possible to work with paper images and paste up news stories and advertisements onto a paper grid.

Such a radical change in production not only entailed careful study of the different set-ups on the market but also called for the printers to acquire new

The revolutionary phototypesetting computer

skills. Long negotiations took place with the unions, which were not all in favour of embracing such big changes. In the event, agreement was reached for the *County Press* to begin using phototypesetting in January, 1978.

But by the end of the year the paper was facing another period of industrial unrest.

On December 4 members of the National Union of Journalists started what developed into a seven-week strike over a pay claim. Although this affected most members of the editorial staff the *County Press* still managed to produce 24-page papers, partly because many readers responded to the editor's request to send in news items.

On April 12, 1980, for the first time in its near-96-year history, the *County Press* failed to appear, a victim of disruptive action by members of the National Graphical Association in pursuit of a national pay and conditions claim. For the first two weeks of the following month the paper was restricted to producing news sheets, after NGA members were suspended without pay. Agreement was then reached between the two sides at national level and normal production resumed.

The paper had a double cause for celebration in October, 1981: the first 44-page paper in its history and the completion of improvements and renovation to 29 High Street. This involved structural repairs, with the Victorian shopfront rebuilt and the reinstatement of the trademark mosaic external panels on the front elevation. Internally the mahogany panelling was refurbished and reinstalled. After the panelling was removed there were tell-tale signs of timbers blackened by a fire but when this occurred remains a mystery.

The news sheet published in April, 1980

It was perhaps a sign of the paper's political independence that the ceremony to mark completion of the £40,000 facelift was performed by the Island's Liberal MP, Mr Stephen Ross – later Lord Ross. He described the *County Press* as a model of moderation and perfectly fair in its presentation of events.

Lord Ross opening the refurbished 29 High Street in October, 1981. Company chairman Lt Col W J Eldridge is holding the umbrella. Next to Mr Bradbeer is his wife, Rosemary

Five weeks later the paper was justly trumpeting another record – a 52-page edition. This booming expansion meant that time was running out for the nearly 30-year-old Crabtree rotary press. The solution was to replace it with a web-offset machine. Linonews, a machine built in Altrincham, was chosen, but the cost meant that the company could afford only seven units of four pages each.

A 28-page section was therefore the largest that could be printed and was why the paper still had to be produced in sections. On the other hand, web-offset brought with it major benefits such as a much higher quality of printing and photographic reproduction and the ability to print colour. The equipment was too large to install in the old printing works in Pyle Street and the directors agreed it should be sited in a factory unit, previously used for boatbuilding, on the Riverway Industrial Estate, about half-a-mile away.

This major change took place in 1985, marking the final phase of a £400,000 investment programme. It led to the paper claiming, not without reason, to having "one of the most modern newspaper printing plants for our size in the country".

The investment in modern technology was rewarded with continued rises in circulation and by August, 1988, new records were being set with weekly average sales in the first six months of the year of 36,182 – an increase of 725 copies weekly over the comparable period the previous year.

And the trend was still upwards. By the July, sales were averaging 37,306. The findings of a survey carried out by a market research organisation, RSGB, showed that 95 percent of Islanders regularly saw the *County Press*, while 84 percent read it every week.

The survey also found that the paper appealed almost equally to all age groups, both sexes and all income groups.

Mr Rea had retired as editor in December, 1987, and was succeeded by Mr Peter Hurst, whose previous experience included editing the *East Grinstead Observer* and the *Surrey Herald Series*.

In October, 1988, a new executive board of directors was appointed to control the *County Press*, which had been reorganised with separate companies formed for the newspaper and printing business and the mainland-based retail stationery group – W J Atkins, the long-established Southampton retail stationers, had been purchased in December, 1980.

Mr Bradbeer was chairman of the holding company and both subsidiaries, while remaining as managing director of Atkins the Stationers Ltd. Mr Robin Freeman, who joined the *County Press* in 1981 as general manager from Westerham Press, in Kent, was appointed managing director of the *County Press*. Mr Tony Thorpe, works manager for six years, became works director and Mr Hurst editorial director.

The removal of printing to the Riverway Industrial Estate paved the way for the redevelopment of the Pyle Street site with the attractive new building that is the home of the *County Press* today – but that is another story, with a strong royal connection, as readers will find later. ◆

The web-offset printing machine installed at a new site on the Riverway Industrial Estate in 1985. On the left is Mark Lawn carrying on a family tradition

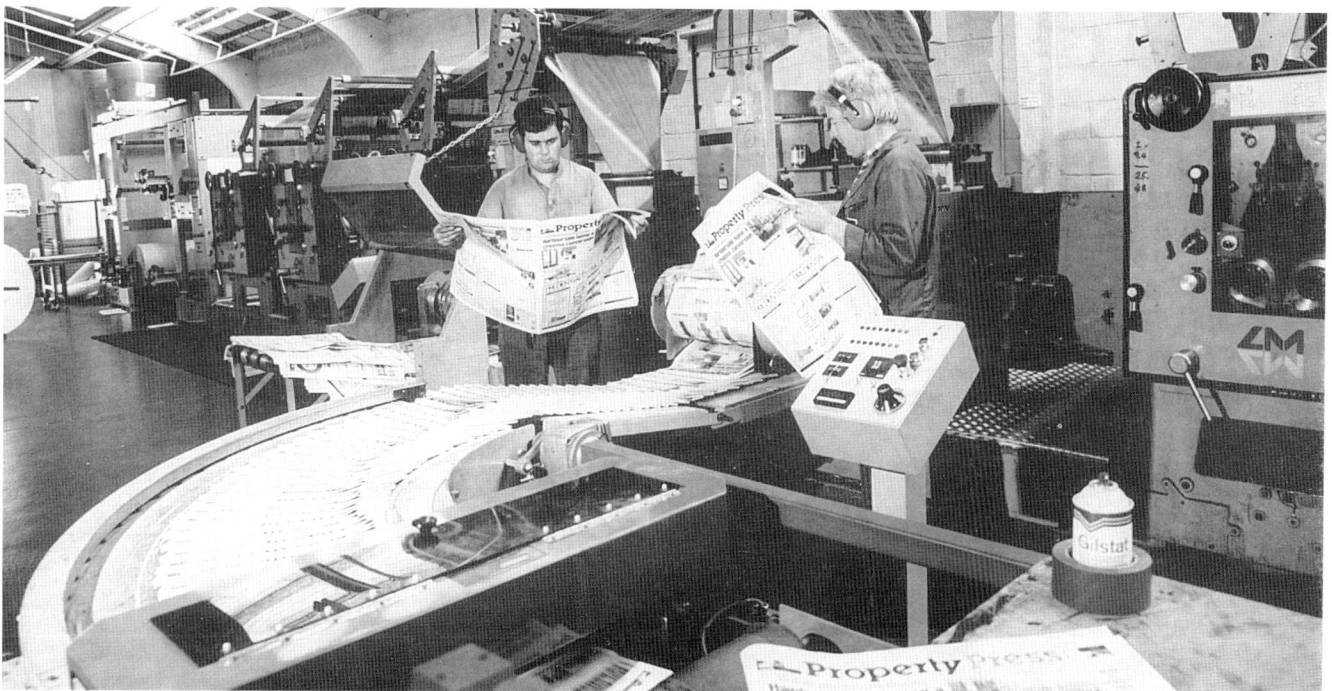

CHAPTER TWO **A FAMILY AFFAIR**

The *County Press* is by no means the only legacy the Island has inherited from the Brannon family. Long before the first edition of the paper appeared in 1884 they were in the communications business. It all started with George Brannon, grandfather of the *County Press* founder, whose reputation as an engraver of Island scenes is unrivalled. As Dr P T Armitage observes in his bibliography of George Brannon's *Vectis Scenery*: "Not only was he responsible for eight major publications about the Isle of Wight but his work laid the foundations for his grandson to become co-proprietor of the *IW County Press*."

George Brannon was born in Ireland, probably in County Antrim, in 1784. The scarcity of records there made it impossible for Dr Armitage to be more precise, but he surmises that George became an apprentice printer. As a young man he moved to London where he met his future wife, Jane Whitford. They married in 1813 and the same year moved to the Island – George had almost certainly visited the Island before and seen its potential for his artistry.

After a brief stay in Newport the couple set up home in Landscape Cottage at Wootton Common, which he later portrayed for posterity in a print. They had nine children, of whom Alfred and Philip are of special interest.

One of George's first engravings of an Island scene, the *Gateway to Carisbrooke Castle*, decorated the cover of a guide book, *Clarke's Delineator of the Isle of Wight*, published about 1818. So more than 60 years before the *County Press* made its debut a Brannon was playing a part in publicising the Island, an activity that found much greater expression in Vectis Scenery.

In the late autumn of 1820 George published, without any text and in a brown wrapper, the first six plates of *Vectis Scenery*. About a year later he published the first complete volume of 28 engravings, still without text, price one guinea. In 1822 he added six pages of description to produce what is basically the publication known by collectors today.

Although moderately successful during the early years of his business, he received a significant boost to his reputation when John Nash, the leading architect, commissioned him to draw and engrave six large pictures of East Cowes Castle. These engravings, examples of which were included in an exhibition of Brannon prints staged to mark the *County Press*'s centenary, were used by Nash to give to his wealthy potential clients as a form of advertising.

There was also a beneficial spin-off for the artist since his work became more sought after and it was at this time that he published other books and travel guides. Among them were *The Pleasure Visitor's Companion* and *Picture of the Isle of Wight*. He carried on his business until 1857, when he retired, aged 73. He was succeeded by his son, Alfred, and continued to draw and engrave for him. George's last two engravings, of the River Yar and Appuldurcombe House, were published after his death in 1860.

Alfred, who married Martha Urry, of Gatcombe, in 1834, was 42 when he took over. As had been the case with his father, engravings of large houses were an important money-spinner. When one such property changed hands and Alfred obtained a commission from the new owner, he was not above using his father's engravings, altering them and substituting his own name and a new date.

Opposite **One of George Brannon's first engravings of an Island scene**

Sales of *Vectis Scenery* – which had been issued every year since 1820 – began to slow down, possibly due to the increasing popularity of photography. Regular annual publication stopped around 1866, although sporadic issues were made as late as 1875.

In 1875 Alfred was partially blinded while cutting some branches at Landscape Cottage and his eldest son, George, then 36, who had been apprenticed to his father as a lithographic printer, had to return from London to run the printing and publishing business, which was then established in Holyrood Street, Newport. As we have seen, this became the platform from which he played such a vital part in the launch of the *County Press* nine years later.

Philip Brannon, one of George Brannon, senior's sons, was born in 1816 and is regarded as the most gifted and versatile member of the clan. At various times he was a painter, engraver, teacher, architect and civil engineer. Among his achievements was the design for the Hartley Institute, forerunner of Southampton University; the foundation of a so-called Ragged School for poor children at Newport; and the design of churches, harbours and bridges in various parts of the country.

Philip even designed an airship, *The Mars*, for the relief of the Siege of Paris in the Franco-Prussian War and invented a new form of fire protection used in St Paul's Cathedral. He also painted several watercolours, several of which were on show in the *County Press* centenary exhibition. Sad to say he died a pauper at Sandown, apparently having frittered his money away on a series of women.

The story of George Brannon junior has been unfolded in the history of the first half-century and more of the *County Press*. So too has that of his son, Wilfrid, a distinguished soldier who succeeded his father in the management of the paper. Both enjoyed great loyalty from their staff because they were natural leaders who earned the respect of their employees for their sense of fair play.

As the paper said in George Brannon's obituary in February, 1938: "It was his child, which he nurtured through the trials of infancy and by exemplary devotion, integrity and sound vision brought to the lusty manhood it enjoys today. As a practical master of his craft he had few peers. No one could possibly have had higher ideals of the service which craftsmanship ought to render to the community and those who have had the privilege of working under his direction, some over the long period of half-a-century, can bear the most sincere testimony to his rare qualities as an employer."

The essence of the man, who was 87 when he died, can also be judged by his many outside interests, including being secretary of the Newport Benevolent Society which met a real need in securing winter supplies of coal at reduced prices for poor families.

Lt Col Wilfrid Brannon carried on as his father left off. But although he was so closely associated with the paper all his life he was also a military man, being the only Islander to rise through the ranks to command Princess Beatrice's IW Rifles (8th Battalion of the Hampshire Regiment, TA). As a young officer during the First World War he served at Gallipoli and in Palestine and was awarded the Military Cross for the way he led an attack on the Turkish trenches.

He continued with the TA after the war and in 1937 as a Lt Col commanding the IW Rifles, which had by then converted to a heavy artillery unit, he became, at 44, the youngest

Islander to be appointed a Deputy Lieutenant for Hampshire and the IW. He continued as a senior Deputy Lieutenant for the Island after local government re-organisation in 1974, when the IW retained its county status and was also granted its own Lord Lieutenant separate from Hampshire – an office Earl Mountbatten assumed in tandem with the governorship.

Col Brannon commanded the IW Heavy Regiment, RA, in World War II and was later seconded for duty on airfield defence with the RAF. In 1944, when he was able to resume his management of the *County Press*, he took command of the East Wight Home Guard.

No one should underestimate his major contribution to the development and continued success of the paper. As a young man he had learned every facet of the business and when employees became embroiled in national industrial disputes he was able to take over operating a type-setting machine. His main aim was that the *County Press* should never miss publication. When he retired from active management in 1959, he was appointed to succeed Mr H R Palmer as chairman of the board, a position which he held at the time of his death, aged 82, in January, 1976.

Today the paper's links with the Brannon family are as close as ever, the chairman of the board, Mr Bradbeer, is married to Rosemary, daughter of Lt Col Brannon and his wife, Audrey. Mr Bradbeer is the son of a dental surgeon from Bovey Tracey, Devon. He met his wife-to-be when he came to Cowes in 1950 as a draughtsman at the J S White's shipyard, after studying naval architecture at Kings College, Newcastle-upon-Tyne and Durham University. Four years later he moved to Brooke Marine, Lowestoft, as assistant yard manager, but in 1955 was persuaded by Col Brannon to join the *County Press* as assistant works manager to Mr George Moth.

He was seconded for a year to the *Western Gazette*, at Yeovil, Somerset, to prepare him for his new career. He succeeded Mr Moth as works manager in 1959, becoming a director of the company in 1969 and general manager two years after. He was appointed managing director in 1973 and took over as company chairman in 1987, combining that role with his managerial responsibilities for six years before handing over the reins of the latter to Mr Robin Freeman, who became group chief executive and managing director.

Mr Bradbeer has followed in the tradition of the Brannon family in guiding the company through some of the most testing times in its history, including industrial problems stemming from national disputes, the pivotal challenge to the *County Press* mounted by the former *IW Weekly Post* and the need to invest significant sums to keep the paper abreast of modern developments in terms of equipment and buildings.

He oversaw the acquisition in December, 1980, of W J Atkins and Son Ltd, the long-established Southampton retail stationers; its expansion into a four-shop operation in and around Southampton; and, as the market in this field changed out of all recognition in a comparatively short time through competition from specialist superstores and other outlets, the disposal of Atkins – completed with the sell-off of the original shop in Southampton in 1997.

As the *County Press* sought to diversify further, Mr Bradbeer also played a leading role in the take-over in October, 1990, of Crossprint, the well-known Newport printing company, which has continued to expand and won a IW Chamber of Commerce Award for Excellence in

1998. He is widely known in yachting circles and has been chairman of Cowes Harbour Commissioners since 1994. In 1997 he was honoured with the appointment as the Island's High Sheriff.

For Mrs Bradbeer the *County Press* has been an inseparable part of her life. When she was born her parents were living in a flat in part of the company's premises at 29 High Street, Newport, and she remembers as a child sitting on the counter handing over the sheets of football results that were posted in the front office windows as soon as they were telephoned in on Saturday afternoons.

She recalls her grandfather, George Brannon, with great affection. "He was a gorgeous man and I always wished I had more time to get to know him better, but he died while I was at boarding school. He and granny celebrated their golden wedding anniversary not long before he died and to my disgust I wasn't allowed to return home for it. I knew my granny much better and I recall being told that she had worked in the ruling room in the First World War."

It was all hands to the pump too when World War II broke out, with Mrs Bradbeer's mother manning a Monotype machine under the watchful eye of Baden Smith, another of those long-serving employees for which the *County Press* is a byword. By that time the family's home was Tenth House in New Road, Wootton, which Col Brannon had designed. But the outbreak of hostilities found his military duties taking him and his wife and daughter to quarters at Totland.

Mrs Bradbeer had joined the paper's front office staff after leaving boarding school and she used to catch an early bus from West Wight to Newport each morning. One of her travelling companions was a reporter named Isabel Allen, daughter of the Vicar of Shalfleet, who in 1946 married the son of a Ventnor jeweller and emigrated to Canada. Details like that are typical of Mrs Bradbeer's encyclopaedic knowledge of *County Press* staff faithfully recorded in journals and cuttings books that reflect her genuine fondness for those who have worked for that larger Brannon family – the *County Press* staff.

She served in the Wrens from 1943 to 1945 and then resumed her duties in the *County Press* front office, where she worked until her marriage. In the immediate post-war years, Mrs Bradbeer recalled her parents used to hold tea parties for the staff at Tenth House which had its own mooring in Wootton Creek. From there her father would take parties out on his motor-cruiser, *Salla*.

She and Mr Bradbeer were understandably proud and delighted when their daughter, Amanda, then 37, was invited to become a *County Press* director in 1997. This great grand-daughter of the *County Press* co-founder is a graduate in accountancy and finance, but her great love is the sea and sailing. She was one of the first two girls to become navigating cadets with the Bank Line and after four years' training and travelling the world on cargo ships gained her second mate's certificate.

Amanda Bradbeer

Above As Chairman of the Isle of Wight County Council, veteran *County Press* employee Keith Lacey was literally on hand throughout Prince Andrew's visit to the Island to open Brannon House and fulfill other engagements

Far left Another view of the scene as Prince Andrew arrived at Brannon House

Left The Prince chats to editor Peter Hurst (centre) and his deputy, Mike Sutcliffe

Above **What caused smiles all round as the Prince met production staff from the Riverway works?**

Right **Deputy Media Manager Mike Rayner discusses a point with the Prince**

Far right **The Prince chats with Sarah Vaughan in the advertising department, while department head Alistair Porteous looks on**

Right **The finale to a memorable day as Prince Andrew unveils the plaque commemorating the opening ceremony**

Further progress in that direction was virtually impossible because of major cutbacks in the British merchant fleet and she became a self-employed yachting instructor, working out of the Hamble School of Yachting. Her latest venture is chartering out her own yacht, a Sigma 38.

Although her career is far removed from the *County Press*, she maintains a close interest in the company through her directorship and, of course, her parents. Of her election to the board, Amanda said: "I was always hoping one day to be appointed and was absolutely thrilled when I was asked. It is nice to continue the family associations with the *County Press*." ◆

CHAPTER THREE **ROYAL CONNECTIONS**

For a rising newspaper like the *County Press* in the closing decades of the last century having Queen Victoria in residence at Osborne House, East Cowes, was heaven-sent. It gave the paper tremendous gravitas when it could report at first hand the day-to-day affairs of the world's greatest monarch who was living in its circulation area. And, of course, the great occasions of state, like the Queen's golden and diamond jubilees and her eventual death at Osborne, were all of global news proportions.

The to-ing and fro-ing of visiting royalty and the joys and grief of royal family life all found their way to the pages of the paper. Osborne had been built 39 years before the *County Press* first appeared and the young Queen and her much loved Consort, Prince Albert, shared only a further 16 happy years before his premature death on December 14, 1861. The effect of that tragedy was graphically illustrated in the award-winning film *Mrs Brown*, but by 1884 Her Majesty had emerged from the reclusive state to which the loss of her husband had driven her.

A year later came a glamorous occasion which in its way was a forerunner of the marvellous spectacle of the marriage of Prince Charles to the then Lady Diana Spencer, the late Diana, Princess of Wales. But in this case the setting for the wedding of Victoria's youngest child, Princess Beatrice, to Prince Henry of Battenberg, was not Westminster Abbey but Osborne's parish church – St Mildred's at nearby Whippingham.

To quote from the *County Press*: "The magnificent spectacle had no parallel in the history of local royal ceremonies. All roads to Whippingham were thronged from an early hour. Stands were erected in the churchyard and in front of the almshouses (opposite the church) for the accommodation of spectators. And so anxious was the Queen that as many as possible should witness the processions from Osborne to the church and back that she gave orders that her cornfields abutting on the route should be thrown open to the public."

The day's events were obviously worth watching. There were 14 carriages for the royal family and other VIPs, including the Prime Minister, Lord Salisbury. The Argyll and Sutherland Highlanders from Parkhurst Barracks and the Island Volunteers provided a guard of honour.

"The bridegroom looked exceedingly handsome in the white uniform of a captain of Cuirassiers of the Prussian Guard and his supporters were the Prince of Bulgaria and Prince Francis Joseph of Battenberg. To the strains of Wagner's Bridal March on the organ the bride, with the Queen Victoria on her left, and her brother, the Prince of Wales, on her right, advanced up the aisle, the Prince of Wales being in the uniform of a field marshal.

"Her Majesty wore a dress of black satin and her jewels included the famous Koh-I-Noor diamond. The Princess Beatrice was charmingly robed in white satin, covered with rich Honiton lace draped with clusters of orange flowers, part of which had figured in the wedding dress of Her Majesty 45 years previously."

Prince Henry of Battenberg and Princess Beatrice on their wedding day in 1885

Opposite **Queen Victoria visiting Newport to celebrate her diamond jubilee in 1897**

The ceremony was performed by the Archbishop of Canterbury and the bride and groom, who occupied the leading carriage on the return to Osborne, were "joyously acclaimed by the huge assemblage". Even the honeymoon was spent on the Island, at Quarr Abbey near Ryde, and Tennyson, the poet laureate, penned a poem in honour of the Princess, at his Farringford, Freshwater, home.

Prince Henry was appointed Governor of the Island in 1889 in a ceremony at Carisbrooke Castle which was to have an echo in the installation into the same office of Earl Mountbatten by the Queen in 1965. When he was not on the Island the Prince kept himself informed of what was happening here through the *County Press*, to which he had been a subscriber since taking over the governorship.

But tragic news came in a telegram to the *County Press* on January 22, 1896, telling of the death of Prince Henry from malaria two days before. It happened while he was serving with the British military expedition to Ashanti, West Africa, for which he had volunteered the previous November. Princess Beatrice and her mother were at Osborne and it was from there that they later made the short journey for the funeral at St Mildred's, grief replacing the joy that had enveloped the church only 11 years before.

During the 17 years of Queen Victoria's record reign covered by the *County Press* she annually spent two extended periods at Osborne – the latter part of the summer season and a considerable part of the winter including Christmas. It became a familiar sight for Islanders to see the Queen being driven around in a carriage drawn by four grey horses, with postilions and outriders and with Indian or Highland attendants in picturesque native dress sitting at the back of the royal carriage.

Naturally the Island was proud to be at the focal point of the greatest empire in the world and to share in some of the most momentous milestones of Victoria's reign. Although the Queen was in London in June, 1887, for national celebrations of her golden jubilee the Island was able to mark it twice.

On Jubilee Day itself, June 21, there were thanksgiving services and towns and villages were en fete, with parties for the aged and poor and for thousands of schoolchildren. At Newport the mayor, Alderman Francis Pittis, laid the foundation stone of the Victoria clock tower at the Guildhall as the Island capital's permanent memorial of the jubilee. Ryde and other towns vied with each other in staging their own celebrations and on her return from London to Osborne the Queen honoured Newport, Ryde and Cowes with a visit at the end of July.

The comprehensive record of these historic happenings filled many pages of the *County Press* and the paper also rose to the occasion by publishing mid-week editions and supplements with the regular weekly editions. The editor, Thomas Lee, received a letter from Sir Henry Ponsonby saying that the Queen had very graciously accepted the account of the jubilee celebrations in the Island that had appeared in the *County Press*.

Ten years later the paper pulled out all the stops again to report the Queen's diamond jubilee – her 60-year reign being longer than any of her predecessors. The poet laureate composed a moving tribute and young and old Islanders were royally entertained. There were decorations and illuminations in towns and villages, climaxed by "brilliant pyrotechnics

Above *County Press* managing director Robin Freeman at the launch in 1996 of the latest bus to publicise the paper. It was the third vehicle from Southern Vectis Omnibus Company to be used for this purpose. On the right is SVOC managing director Alan White

Left Cheers for two of the *County Press*'s star contributors – cartoonist Rupert Besley and columnist Charlotte Hofton. They jointly performed the official re-opening of the Wishing Well pub at Pondwell. On the right is Anthony Goddard, boss of Goddards Brewery, owners of the pub

Right The editorial flair of features editor Ron Kentish and the graphic design expertise of Steve Hookey combined to create this eye-catching front page of the Millennium supplement. Steve was a compositor before retraining on computers, a classic example of a printer learning new skills

INTO THE NEW
MILLENNIUM
with THE ISLE OF WIGHT COUNTY PRESS

Bringing past, present and future alive

The Island's Royal prisoner — Page 8

The Island's Royal resident — Page 9

102 year-old Hilda's century of memories — Pages 12 and 13

Island children's hopes for the 21st century — Pages 10 and 11

Below Web site champion Maurice Bower creating an on line edition of the paper

displays" and the burning of bonfires on the downs. Just as she had done on her golden jubilee, the Queen made official visits to the Island's three main towns.

New jubilee florins were distributed to the elderly and some 3,500 children marched to Carisbrooke Castle for tea and sports on the historic bowling green, where Charles I once played. The celebrations had a grand finale in the great naval review at Spithead, a salutary reminder of the past in these days when there are more admirals than warships in the Royal Navy! People thronged the Island's northern shores to view the massive fleet, which looked even more spectacular at night when all the ships were illuminated.

One can imagine the planning and extra workload all this entailed for the *County Press* staff. The diary detailing reporters' engagements often resembled a court circular and they must have been the envy not only of their provincial contemporaries but many in Fleet Street. What stories they had to tell their children and grandchildren of the days when covering royal assignments were routine and not the once-in-a-lifetime event they are for most weekly journalists . . .

In July, 1899, the Queen opened the new children's ward of the County Hospital at Ryde – later the Royal IW County Hospital – which, with the endowment of five cots at £1,000 each, was the Island's official memorial of the diamond jubilee. The £9,738 fund publicly subscribed for the ward and its endowment was substantially boosted by donations contributed through a Shilling Fund subscribed by *County Press* readers.

The Victoria Recreation Ground was Newport's own diamond jubilee tribute to the Queen, while Cowes saw the opening on the seafront of Victoria Parade and at Ryde a new organ was installed in the town hall.

Although no-one would have mentioned it at the time, it must have been on many minds that the end of the Queen's extraordinary reign, which began in 1837, could not be far off. It was on Tuesday, January 22, 1901, at 6.45pm, that the fateful message was posted at the Prince of Wales Gate at Osborne: "Her Majesty the Queen breathed her last at 6.30pm, surrounded by her children and grandchildren."

Newspapermen from all over the world had been waiting outside Osborne for the news and the author recalls being told by a former *County Press* editor, Mr Walter Sibbick, how one canny local reporter beat them all to the story. He took up position in the nearest telephone box and when he saw the horde of reporters rushing towards him promptly flashed the news of the Queen's death to a Fleet Street agency. The *County Press*, of course, received prompt news of Victoria's passing and published a special edition the same evening, displaying again the remarkable all-round professionalism of its editorial and production staff.

Queen Victoria

The Prince of Wales, who became King Edward VII on his mother's death, attended a service at St Mildred's, Whippingham, the following Sunday with Queen Alexandra. Among other royals present were the German Emperor, the German Crown Prince, the Duke and Duchess of Cornwall and of York, the Duchess of Saxe-Coburg and Gotha, Princess Henry of Battenberg (Princess Beatrice) and her children and Prince and Princess Christian and Princess Victoria of Schleswig-Holstein.

The funeral ceremonial began on February 1 when the Island witnessed the stately and majestic pageant of the removal of Queen Victoria from her Island home on the first stage of the journey to her final resting place at Frogmore, Windsor, where the remains of her husband had been taken nearly 40 years before. In a graphic scene-setter the *County Press* told of how the funeral procession from Osborne to Trinity Pier, East Cowes, "while dignified beyond all local precedent, had a home-like character and was definitely affecting".

It continued: "The royal and other exalted mourners proceeded on foot from Osborne to East Cowes pier. Assuredly such a 'walking' funeral had never before been recorded in history. To the roll of many muffled drums, the royal coffin was placed on board the Queen's yacht *Alberta*, the quarter-deck of which had been furnished as a chapel. Just before 3pm the *Alberta* moved off with the mortal remains of its royal mistress, slowly steaming between the double line of huge battleships representing the naval power of Britain, Germany, France, Japan and other friendly nations."

So the curtain came down on what until then had been the most important period in the Island's history, certainly in terms of being at the centre of national events. The *County Press* can take justifiable pride in the way it responded to the challenge, as it became an increasingly confident and highly competent newspaper, showing a flair and ingenuity that today's editorial team recognises as deserving of the highest praise.

Acknowledging local sympathy, Princess Beatrice, who had succeeded her late husband as Governor of the Island, said: "It will indeed be a help to me when setting up my new home in your midst to know that I am amongst those who loved and revered my dear mother, who did so much for the Island." The Governor's new home was at Osborne Cottage and later at Carisbrooke Castle. Her long and faithful tenure continuing until her death in 1944.

Not surprisingly, St Mildred's, Whippingham, with its many associations with Queen Victoria, was chosen by the King and the Royal Family as the most suitable place for their memorial to her. This took the form of the enlargement and adornment of the chancel, including the erection of a beautiful carved white marble reredos, representing the Last Supper.

Having been at the forefront of the final days of the old Queen, the Island was centre-stage again in the lead-up to the coronation of the new King. This was originally fixed for June 26, 1902, but had to be dramatically postponed when King Edward was taken seriously ill and had to have an operation. Three weeks after the operation the *County Press* reported that His Majesty had arrived at Cowes on the Royal Yacht *Victoria and Albert*. Then: "On August 6, in the middle of Cowes Week, the King was well enough to return to London for the coronation, which took place on August 9 and Islanders found a great reason for gratification in the knowledge that the healthful breezes of the Solent had contributed largely to His Majesty's complete restoration to health."

But the change in the monarchy also marked the end of the Island having the head of state regularly in its midst. On Coronation Day the King announced in a letter to the Prime Minister his decision to give the Osborne Estate to the nation – when he was not in London or Windsor he enjoyed his strong ties with Norfolk and had no need for a home on the Island. The King said that as Osborne was sacred to the memory of his mother he wished, with the exception of those apartments she had personally occupied, for the public to have access to the house which would for ever be associated with her.

The Island's beautiful memorial to Queen Victoria, erected in St James's Square, Newport, was unveiled on August 13, 1903, by Princess Beatrice and then for many years future Island links with Royalty were centred on Cowes Week. Early in August, 1909, the *County Press* was reporting on the Russian Imperial yacht, *Standard*, arriving in Cowes Roads with the Czar, Czarina and their children aboard. It was the first and last visit of the Russian Imperial family, tragic victims of the Russian Revolution a few years later.

In contrast to his mother's long reign, Edward VII's lasted only just over nine years. News of his death shortly before midnight on May 6, 1910, reached the *County Press* by wire just after the first edition had been printed. A second edition was speedily produced and the paper was able to give Islanders the first written announcement. An ophthalmic-ward at the County Hospital was the Island memorial to the late King.

His successor, George V, and Queen Mary were no strangers to the Island and while still Prince and Princess of Wales had spent short periods at Barton Manor, near Osborne, which King Edward had retained. In 1897 the Prince of Wales had become Colonel of the Isle of Wight Rifles. The new King and and his Queen paid their first official visit to the Island on July 23, 1910, and through the years Cowes Week was regularly honoured by the presence of George V aboard his magnificent yacht *Britannia*, a 122ft. racing cutter, which was scuttled, in accordance with his wishes, after his death in 1936.

Part of the fascination of compiling the history of the *County Press* are the unexpected sequels that arise many years later. Thus, in the early 1990s we reported how Mr Martin Woodward, the coxswain of Bembridge lifeboat and a noted diver, discovered the wreck of the *Britannia* after a fisherman friend's gear was caught up in it in St Catherine's Deep, south of Ventnor. Plans were mooted by a consortium to raise the yacht, but Mr Woodward distanced himself from such an operation because it would have been against the late King's wishes; in any case he thought the whole enterprise would have been impossible.

While her husband was sailing, Queen Mary used to occupy her time on tours of the Island – sometimes going to antique shops and more regularly to Blackgang Chine. Mr Dick Dabell, whose family is famous for turning the chine into a major tourist attraction, said that the Queen used to watch *Britannia* and other yachts passing Blackgang. He recalled how she used to tap him under the chin and say, "Nice little boy," and of how she used to buy gifts from the chine's bazaar, which were then sent off to Buckingham Palace. "Once her hat was knocked off by the jaw of the whale skeleton and we had to saw a bit off to try to make sure it didn't happen again," said Mr Dabell.

Queen Mary draws a crowd on a visit to an antique shop at Bembridge

He also told of the tense time his father had whenever the Royal visitor was at the chine. "He had been deafened in the First World War and as there were no deaf aids in those days he had to watch the Queen's facial expressions to decided whether to say 'Yes' or 'No' to her questions. If she put on a pained expression after he had replied he knew he had got it wrong, or that is how family legend has it."

Anecdotes like this show that through Queen Mary the Island and its faithful reporter, the *County Press*, had regained to some extent the close royal links treasured in Queen Victoria's time. Devotion to the Royal Family was given full play on July 22, 1926, when the Prince of Wales – Edward VIII to be – paid an official visit. He too knew the Island well through youthful days at Osborne, where he was a cadet after it became a naval college and through yachting at Cowes.

Only with hindsight in the light of the Abdication crisis ten years later can we see the unconscious irony of the *County Press* report of his visit. "Large numbers thronged the route of the popular Prince's 60 miles' triumphal tour round the Island and acclaimed the Heir-Apparent with the loyal fervour which his magnificent record of service and irresistible personal charm assured for him." His crowded itinerary that day included the new marine drive and promenade, appropriately named Prince's Esplanade, linking Cowes and Gurnard.

King George VI, who succeeded Edward VIII in 1936, visited the Island two years later and went to Osborne House accompanied by Queen Elizabeth and the present Queen, then Princess Elizabeth – an occasion recalled by the Queen Mother when in the summer of 1975 she toured Ventnor Botanic Garden; attended a dedication service at St Lawrence Church of two stained glass windows from the chapel of the former Royal National Hospital of which she was the last royal patron, and opened a housing project for the mentally handicapped at East Cowes, named in her honour Glamis Court.

Yachting inevitably played its part in the Island's link with the present Queen even before she ascended to the throne in 1952. When she married Prince Philip in 1948 the Island Sailing Club presented the royal newlyweds with a Dragon Class racing yacht named, rather controversially, *Bluebottle*.

Prince Philip sailing during Cowes Week

Just how unhappy some people were at this was expressed in a letter to the *County Press* from Boat Lover of Wootton, who wrote: "I read with amazement that the Princess's yacht is to be called *Bluebottle*. A Dragon is a creation of delicate strength and beauty, the pride of the boat-builder's art. To christen one after a frequenter of dung heaps and decayed meat appears to me appalling." Boat Lover of Wootton (could this have been the non de plume of the CP's manager Lt Col Brannon?) was probably happier with the apt name – *Coweslip* – given to a Flying Fifteen that was the wedding gift to the royal couple from the people of Cowes.

Through Prince Philip's love of yachting Cowes Week regained the prestige of royal patronage and the attendant national and international publicity that accompanies it. The Prince formed a close friendship with one of the Island's great characters Uffa Fox, the famous Cowes helmsman and boat designer, who also taught Prince Charles the sailing ropes.

The four royal children, Prince Charles, Princess Anne,

Prince Andrew and Prince Edward followed in their father's wake. Incidentally, Princess Anne, now the Princess Royal, has become the most frequent Royal visitor to the Island, fostering various good causes like the Save the Children Fund and Riding for the Disabled.

There was dancing in the streets, or rather St James's Square, Newport, to celebrate the coronation of Queen Elizabeth II in June, 1953, but it was the naval review in Spithead which brought the spectacular finale of the celebrations to the Island's doorstep.

Needless to say, Cowes Week always receives comprehensive coverage in words and pictures from the

Dancing in St James's Square to celebrate the coronation of Queen Elizabeth II

County Press. Until her withdrawal from service the Royal Yacht *Britannia* served as a floating home for members of the family and their guests at the great yachting festival. No-one who saw it will forget the scenes as *Britannia* made her final departure from Cowes Week in 1996, graphically captured by *County Press* chief photographer Chris Thwaites from a vantage point in the tower of Holy Trinity Church.

For the *County Press*, July 26 and 27, 1965, will go down as a milestone in its and the Island's history. The then chief reporter, the late Leslie Longhurst, was given the exacting but rewarding task of reporting on the Queen's first official visit here. The main engagement was the installation of Admiral of the Fleet Earl Mountbatten of Burma as Governor of the Island in the regal setting of Carisbrooke Castle. As Leslie Longhurst wrote of the two-day visit: "This was not only a great honour for the Island, it was also an historic and memorable occasion. Her Majesty's visit renewed long-cherished associations of the Royal House with the Isle of Wight and it was the culmination of the long-cherished and oft-expressed hopes of her Island people."

Adding to the splendour of the visit, Her Majesty and Prince Philip stayed aboard *Britannia* off Cowes and used the royal barge to visit Newport and Yarmouth. Their tour included Westland's and Osborne House, Ryde, Sandown, Shanklin and Ventnor, and ended on a highly newsworthy note as the Queen left for the mainland in a Westland SRN5 military-type hovercraft.

It was Her Majesty's first trip in a hovercraft – the revolutionary craft capable of travelling over sea and land, invented by Sir Christopher Cockerell and developed on the Island. But embarrassingly for the Interservice Hovercraft Trials Unit from Lee-on-the-Solent, the SRN5 broke down before reaching Thorney Island and the Queen had to complete her cross-Solent trip by naval launch . . .

The Queen hands the scroll of office to the new Governor, Earl Mountbatten

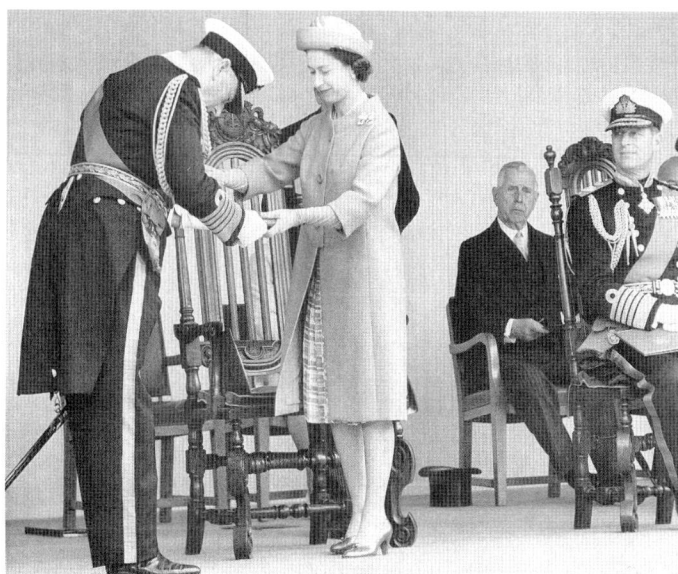

So for the Island began the Mountbatten Years, with its Governor one of Britain's most acclaimed wartime commanders and the former Viceroy and Governor-General who had paved the way for the epic partition of India. Earl Mountbatten, who succeeded the Duke of Wellington into the historic office, brought with him too the added prestige of being a member of the Royal Family. He was uncle of Prince Philip and widely regarded as a mentor to Prince Charles. There were close personal ties too with the governorship, his uncle, Prince Henry of Battenberg, also having held the post.

Although then calling himself an 'Overner', as a child Earl Mountbatten lived with his parents at Kent House on the Osborne Estate. As Honorary Colonel of the 428 HAA Regiment, RA, TA (Princess Beatrice's Isle of Wight Rifles), the new Governor had already established a latter-day Island connection and despite many national calls on his time was no mere figurehead. On the contrary, as the files of the *County Press* show, he was regularly on the Island fulfilling a crowded programme. Whether planting a tree, opening a new building, or visiting a factory, his panache, ability to put everyone at their ease and genuine interest in all he met and saw, endeared him to Islanders. It must have been a matter of great pride for him too when he welcomed the Queen, Prince Charles and Prince Andrew on a visit to the British Hovercraft Factory, East Cowes, in 1968.

In 1974 at another colourful Carisbrooke Castle ceremony, Earl Mountbatten became Lord Lieutenant of the Island, following creation of the post when the Island won its fight to keep its county status. He was made the first honorary freeman of the Borough of Medina in March, 1979, an act which was described as conferring on him the status of "a true Islander".

The savagery with which Earl Mountbatten's life was ended five months later, by an IRA bomb in the Irish Republic, left an indelible mark on the Island as well as the world at large. Five thousand Islanders gathered at Carisbrooke Castle for an open-air memorial service and to pay their last tribute. As the *County Press* reported: "It brought together people of all kinds wishing to honour someone who was described to them as 'a very uncommon man'."

When Prince Charles unveiled a bronze bust of Earl Mountbatten in a crowded St James's Square at Newport, in June, 1982, he spoke of the great affection in which the late Governor had been held. During the hugely successful visit the Prince also officially opened the £3 million Mountbatten Centre at Newport, comprising a trend-setting high school and community facilities – a concept which he held up as an example for the rest of the country to follow.

Front page colour photographs gave added impact to the *County Press* coverage of the visit by the Queen and Prince Philip to Ryde on May 15, 1987. By this time royal walkabouts had become the vogue. The Queen received masses of bouquets and posies from well-wishers and Prince Philip gave photographers one of the shots of the day as he picked up a small girl from behind a barrier and introduced her to Her Majesty. "One of many magic moments," as our reporter said.

The Royal couple had sailed from Portsmouth to see a replica fleet of square riggers assembled in the Solent in readiness for retracing the sailing of the First Fleet to Australia 200 years before. At Ryde the Queen spoke of her pleasure at being associated with the bicentenary celebrations at Portsmouth and on the Island. She unveiled a plaque at Ryde in the St Thomas's Church garden of rest and then, with Prince Philip, saw the British-Australian Heritage Society exhibition in the former St Thomas's Church.

Unlike one national tabloid which devoted its entire front page to the episode, the *County Press* briefly told of how marksmen using rifles had shot nine pigeons that had evaded all efforts to evict them from St Thomas's before the Royal visit . . .

No review of the Island's royal associations would be complete without reference to the late Diana, Princess of Wales. Her own family, the Spencers, had historic connections with Ryde. These date from the early 19th century when Ryde's proximity to Portsmouth made it a favourite spot for senior members of the Admiralty. An ancestor of the Princess, the second Earl Spencer, First Lord of the Admiralty between 1794 and 1801, built Westfield House on the western outskirts of Ryde, now converted into flats. The family also founded the forerunner of Green Mount Primary School in what later became known as the Vectis Hall in Melville Street.

Many Islanders had taken the Princess to their hearts long before she made her first official visit to the IW in June, 1985. That affection was strengthened when they met her in the flesh, her ready smile and engaging personality captivating everyone. *County Press* reporters and photographers were out in force for the event, which included touching scenes as the Princess toured the £1 million Adelaide Court and Adelaide Club complex for the elderly at Ryde.

The warm and sunny weather that day was in contrast to the biting wind and bitter cold in December, 1988, when she was back on the Island. But the warmth of the greeting the Princess received at Cowes and her response, raised the temperature psychologically if not physically. At the FBM shipyard she launched a new HM Customs cutter and took the opportunity to support the efforts of the customs and other agencies in the fight against drugs.

Princess Diana during a walkabout on Cowes Parade in December, 1988

In the tragic aftermath of the Princess's death in a car crash in Paris, the *County Press* of September 5, 1997, recalled in words and pictures her unforgettable visits to the Island. Floral tributes were spontaneously placed around the war memorial in St Thomas's Square at Newport and civic leaders led the Island's homage at a service in St Thomas's Church. On the day of the funeral, a variety of events all over the county were cancelled and shops and businesses pulled down their shutters as the nation bade farewell to its beloved Princess. The *County Press* poignantly caught the mood with a picture and story about eight-year-old Zoe Jones as she laid flowers around Newport's war memorial. "I will miss her so much," she told our reporter.

Prince Charles made a memorable visit to the Island in July, 1999, when, as chief reporter Suzanne Pert wrote, he won the hearts of Islanders after breaking from his tight schedule to go on several impromptu walkabouts, including chatting to schoolchildren waiting to greet him outside Osborne House. Crowds packed St James's Square, Newport, the most publicly accessible stop in a six-venue whistlestop tour. In the square a showcase of Prince's Trust-funded Island projects clearly impressed him and he learned at first hand how the fund he inspired had helped change the lives of young people taking part.

The royal day-tripper went to GKN Westland Aerospace, East Cowes; officially opened the new hi-tech headquarters of Pascall Electronic's at Westridge, Ryde; toured Osborne House, and visited the Earl Mountbatten Hospice, Newport, named after his great-uncle. Prince Charles also made a private visit to St Mildred's Church, Whippingham, where he spent some minutes alone before the grave of his paternal great-grandparents, Prince Louis of Battenberg and Princess Victoria of Hesse, at which he laid flowers.

With a front page story and pictures and three other pages packed with pictures and reports, the *County Press* provided all-embracing coverage of the day with a flair and professionalism that undoubtedly would have gained the admiration of staff from yesteryear who reported so comprehensively on the activities of Queen Victoria. ◆

Prince Charles during a walkabout in Newport in July, 1999

CHAPTER FOUR **SERVING THE COMMUNITY**

The affinity that exists between the *County Press* and the Island community is the envy of many other newspapers. The author has seen this at first-hand both as a reporter for the paper and when based on the Island working for a mainland evening newspaper.

As evening paper journalists I and my colleagues did our best to scoop the *County Press* and with the advantage of publishing six days a week that should not have been too difficult. But each Friday the arrival of the CP showed just how many good stories we had missed.

This underlined not only what a first rate editorial team the paper had and has, but also the unique relationship between the *County Press* and its readers, examples of which I was to see repeatedly on rejoining its staff after my evening paper closed its Newport office. If anything important happens on the Island it is not long before someone is ringing in to tell the *County Press* about it. This rapport, added to the unrivalled contacts reporters and village correspondents have throughout the county, means that little of note fails to make the columns of the CP.

The bond between paper and community is a two-way affair. On the one hand it is a priceless asset for the paper to have so many volunteer 'reporters' spread Islandwide and a population ready to open its doors to *County Press* journalists in times of joy and grief. On the other, Islanders know they can turn to the paper for help in time of need, to highlight an injustice, however great or small. It has become an unofficial Ombudsman, often called on as a last resort by someone in desperate straits.

Airing a grievance can go a long way to relieving an individual's frustration as well as being a conduit for putting wrongs right. Hardly a week goes by without an example of this, be it a complaint against heavy-handed bureaucracy or perhaps a tenant who feels he is being unfairly treated by a landlord. These sort of stories are meat and drink to a newspaper. Not only do they make for absorbing reading but they also demonstrate how it serves the community as a champion ready to take on the-powers-that-be on behalf of an individual or a group.

The letters pages of the paper are another indication to the way Islanders rely on their county newspaper, in this case to put forward their points of view on issues of the day or to cross swords in print with other correspondents.

In the final decades of the 20th century the *County Press* noticeably changed from being a paper of record to one that, while continuing to fill this role, also recognised the importance of investigative journalism – not, I hasten to add, of the cheque book kind which has brought sections of the national press into disrepute. No matter how much national and local government pay lip service to an open society, they are never as transparent as they would have the public believe. News management and spin-doctors are anathema to a free Press and the CP has repeatedly shown itself willing and able to cut through ambiguity and half-truths to put the record straight.

Officialdom doesn't like it but it is not this paper's ambition to court popularity in the corridors of power. Respect, yes, but not a cosy relationship that inhibits freedom of expression. Of course, since ceasing in the early 1970s to be registered as a supporter of the

Conservative Party, the paper has often found itself accused of being pro this party or that: a sure sign it is steering a healthy independent course. Only through such a policy can it retain the trust of its readers.

An extraordinary example of how a paper and community can work as one was the *County Press* sponsored appeal for an MRI scanner for St Mary's Hospital at Newport. An appeal to raise £500,000 towards the purchase of this high-tech life-saving equipment was launched in the autumn of 1994 by the *County Press* with a £5,000 donation, matched by £5,000 from Lloyds Bank. By July, 1998, an astonishing £640,000 had been raised towards the £1.1 million bill for the diagnostic imaging equipment. That sum was to rise to more than £650,000 as money continued to come in even after the appeal was officially closed. It was the biggest fund-raising effort the Island has yet seen.

Peter Hurst, who was editor when the appeal was launched and was chairman of the appeal committee, said that in advertising terms the space given to the appeal in the newspaper was worth well over £100,000 – week-to-week coverage keeping it constantly in the public eye. Features editor Ron Kentish, who oversaw that comprehensive coverage and also served on the appeal committee, wrote a vivid account in tribute to the massive, collective fund-raising effort.

County Press chairman Richard Bradbeer performing the opening ceremony for the MRI Scanner

"You walked the Wight, rowed the Solent, jumped out of aeroplanes, swam, ran in gruelling triathlons . . . and even cycled to Paris. You pushed hospital trolleys through the streets, joined the London Marathon, put on fancy dress, had your heads shaved and wore a dog collar for ten weeks. In a hundred and one weird, wonderful and heart-warming different ways you set about raising money for the Island's own vital MRI scanner. In short", enthused Ron, "you were magnificent!"

But he pointed out that behind all the fun and physical effort of fund-raising everyone was only too well aware of the deeply serious reason for the appeal. Until the scanner came on line at St Mary's, Island patients either had to rely on a mobile scanner or travel to mainland hospitals for the service. As Mr Hurst said at the appeal launch: "Lives can be saved, sick and worried patients relieved of their anxiety and medical resources put to better use if the Island has its own MRI scanner."

The honour of performing the opening ceremony fell to *County Press* chairman Richard Bradbeer, who described it as "a wonderful day for the Island's medical services." He added:

"When Peter Hurst first brought this project to the board I think I, along with most of my colleagues, did not really believe what he was trying to do and I was totally sceptical about the whole thing. But he persuaded us, because he is that kind of chap, that it would be successful – and it has been astonishingly successful."

Mr Bradbeer said the fact that the appeal had outstripped its original £500,000 target by so much was a truly remarkable commentary on all the people of the Island who had dug so deeply into their pockets and held so many different events to raise funds for the appeal. Typical of the spirit of the occasion, consultant Dr Peter Close, the appeal's vice-chairman, said that after the efforts people had made to obtain the scanner, he guaranteed it would be used to give a service that was as good as, if not better than, that provided anywhere. Mr Allan Munds, IW Healthcare NHS Trust chairman, summed it up this way: "Frankly, without the help of the *County Press*, being as it is at the heart of the community, we would never have got where we are today."

This was a spectacular example of the paper working with the community, but throughout the years there have been numerous occasions when it has given a helping hand to a deserving cause or individual, whether by sponsorship, donations or gifts in kind, such as printing or discounts on advertising. To mention IW Healing Arts, which does such good work among patients at St Mary's Hospital and in the community, the IW Youth Trust that is of great support to young people, and the IW Rural Community Council's Village Ventures scheme, gives a general idea of the kind of organisations the *County Press* helps.

The recently launched *County Press* drama awards for Island amateur theatrical companies, the annual carol competition jointly organised with the Tritone Singers and support for the Island's International Oboe Competition are other examples. So too are cricket and sportsmanship awards, the annual junior tennis tournament, the IW Best Kept Village competition and the art competition that has provided the added benefit of splendid illustrations for the CP calendar. The paper has also joined in the fight against crime through the Crime Desk and the Crimestoppers initiatives and has hosted coffee mornings as part of a national fundraiser for the Macmillan Cancer Relief appeal.

For Christmas, 1998, readers gave a heart-warming response to an appeal for toys for disadvantaged children, jointly organised with the IW Directorate of Social Services. A total of 120 Island youngsters benefited, each receiving a sackful of toys and games delivered by a team of social workers. That still left 50 sacks of toys to be sent to children in Romania and Chernobyl. And May, 1999, saw the *County Press* playing its part as co-sponsor with Red Funnel Ferries in presenting Islanders and visitors with a magnificent pre-Chelsea flower show in the grounds of Osborne House – an estimated 15,000 attending an event which will surely become a hardy annual on the Island calendar. ◆

CHAPTER FIVE **ADVERTISING**

Isle of Wight County Press

There are no half measures when it comes to advertisements. Depending on whether you work in the advertising or editorial departments, the space between the adverts has been graciously left on a page for news by those who earn the paper's bread and butter, or it is the reason why editors are constantly trying to fit a quart into a pint pot or whatever is the metric equivalent. Realistically, the advertisements cannot do without news and vice versa. This is particularly evident on the *County Press* where its reputation for news coverage and as an advertising medium are held in equally high regard.

If you want to sell or buy a house or car; find out what is on at the cinema or theatre; let people know you are launching a new business; choose where to go for a meal, or look for a bargain in the classified columns you will almost certainly need to go no further than the pages of the *County Press*. The dilemma for those in charge is to get the balance between news and advertising right. The temptation to allow advertising to gobble up the columns is obvious, bearing in mind that income from this source accounts for about 75 per cent of the revenue for a paper like the *County Press*.

In balancing the financial interests of the company and the demands of advertisers with the need to provide a comprehensive news service, management works on the basis of allocating 60 percent of the paper to advertising and the remainder to news.

Readers may well ask what happens to the money they pay for their copy of the paper. The answer is that a proportion goes to the wholesaler for distribution, and another part goes to the newsagents for filling their invaluable role in selling and delivering the paper. What is left pays for the expensive newsprint on which the CP is produced and some of the production costs.

The growth of advertising supplements has been one of the most significant developments in recent times. As well as generating extra income these also provide interesting articles for readers, ranging in subject from weddings and home improvements to motoring and property. Thanks to the expertise of features editor Ron Kentish and the creativity of the advertising and production department, *County*

A special supplement for Cowes Week produced in August, 1999

Isle of Wight County Press Souvenir Guide
July 31 – August 7, 1999

COWES WEEK
Cowes Week
Skandia Life

32 Page Special Regatta Week Supplement
● Cowes fashion ashore and afloat – pages 8, 9, 10 and 11   **PLUS** – Chance to win prizes in our
● Full guide to action afloat – pages 30 and 31   Pimm's competition – page 28

Press supplements have become a byword for flair – attractively combining the role of informing the reader and selling the product. Advertorials, as they are called in the trade, are another way in which advertising and editorial resources are deployed side by side.

For many years working in the *County Press* advertising department was virtually a one-way affair – processing requests from customers, with little need to try and attract new business. Nowadays, the department is a vibrant, go-getting organisation fully adjusted to coping with competition for business from radio, television and other publications. "We are out there in the market place selling to and servicing our customers and always on the lookout for anything new that is happening," was how advertising manager Alistair Porteous put it. "The seeds of the change were sown when we were in the old building about 12 years ago, but of course the new technology that we have in Brannon House gives us the ability to do so much more. Through our liaison with the editorial department we are also able to place greater emphasis on offering a complete package."

The department is neatly divided into three: the reception staff who deal with customers' copy over the counter, telesales, and sales and marketing. An example of how the work of advertising staff has expanded and diversified came in 1998 when sales and marketing took over the organisation and promotion of an Island Motor Show. An imaginative supplement helped set the scene and dealers and their customers voted the event a great success, confirmed by the decision to repeat it. *Holiday News*, the colourful and informative tabloid-sized paper given away free to visitors and locals, is yet another example of the way the company responds to the needs of readers and advertisers.

Just as the *County Press* is proud of the loyalty of its readers, so too it takes pride in the close relationships it has with advertisers. Some firms have been using its pages to sell their products or services since the very first edition of the paper, while others carried on until their business closed down, like Wadham's, the Newport furnishers, or their identify was lost when taken over, like W B Mew, Langton and Co, the Newport brewers. Mew Langton director Mr Leonard Mew was a member of the *County Press* board.

Among those advertisers whose names appeared in the maiden issue of the paper in 1884 and are immediately recognisable today are estate agents Sir Francis Pittis and Son, timber merchants H W Morey and Son and the Globe Hotel on The Parade at Cowes. Older Islanders will remember the names of other businesses which promoted their products on the front page of the first *County Press*, such as Jordan and Stanley, the grocers, and J E Snellgrove and Son, plumbers, glaziers, paper-hangers and general decorators.

Advertisers in those days did not have to worry about the Trades Description Act. I wonder if the "extra-ordinary power" of Hewett's "celebrated Tamarind Drops" were as effective as the makers claimed in "immediately relieving and eventually curing the most obstinate coughs, colds, hoarseness, bronchitis and difficulty with breathing." But in the words of the advertisement for Professor J Hobbs, of the Botanic and Electric Dispensary, in Pyle Street, Newport, and High Street, Ryde: "Health is wealth" – a happy state no doubt assisted by Hobbs' wonderful composition powder, anti-spasmodic tincture, or celebrated dandelion and general family pills.

Having been co-founded by printer George Brannon, the *County Press* maintained a commercial or jobbing printing department until mid-1992 and even for several years after that continued to produce yachting's *Solent Year Book* and magazines for model railway locomotive builders and model car enthusiasts. Someone who gave sterling service on this side of the business was the late Percy Appel, who began his apprenticeship in 1913 and soon afterwards transferred to the jobbing department. He recalled his long career in the paper's centenary supplement. "Before the 1914-18 war all the typesetting was done entirely by hand by compositors," said Mr Appel. "We had to do the corrections and handle the distribution too, with a weekly wage averaging about £1."

Later came Intertype and Monotype machines to speed the setting process. Quarterly booklets for the Seismological Society listing the world's earthquakes were among long-standing contracts and in the 1920s the *County Press* became the first Island firm to produce bus timetables. Printing of a holiday guide for the IW Publicity Council, whose office was in the CP building, was a major contract after the Second World War, as the Island tourist industry enjoyed a post-war revival. The introduction of modern machines to meet the much greater use of colour ensured that the department could maintain its reputation for high-quality production, including eye-catching brochures for hotels and other holiday businesses.

Mr Appel, noted for his twinkling eyes and cheery grin, was foreman of the jobbing department from 1945 until retirement from full-time employment in 1963, but in the tradition of *County Press* stalwarts carried on working a further 11 years part-time to complete 61 years in total with the company. For many years there was also a small bookbinding department, where the late Jack Coombes, an employee for well over half-a-century, practised this specialist craft and passed on his know-how to young colleagues. Mr Coombes, a fine fast bowler and a stalwart of *County Press* cricket teams, retired from full-time work at the age of 65 and then continued part-time until finally retiring in 1982 after 58 years with the firm.

As a group the *County Press* still has a direct link with printing through the take-over in October, 1990, of Crossprint, of Newport, a design and print company specialising in magazines, corporate literature and brochures.

While the company sold items of stationery over the front office counter it did not have a shop until one was built as part of Brannon House. Since then, under the enthusiastic managership of David Owen, this has established itself as an outlet for quality stationery, writing accessories and many other attractive items and as the place to go for new books about the Island. The shop serves another useful purpose by taking advertisements on Saturdays when the office is closed and is active as a ticket agency for major Island events. Mr Owen has also become a familiar figure at major Island gatherings, like the Newchurch Garlic Festival, when he takes the shop on the road. ◆

CHAPTER SIX **THE LAWNS**

The *County Press* is a family firm in more ways than one. We have already traced its indelible and continuing links with the Brannon family and it is not an exaggeration to say that this has set the pattern. There are numerous examples of a son and a daughter following in father's or mother's footsteps, and, incidentally, quite a few husbands and their wives have been on the payroll too.

A remarkable example of the family tradition are the Lawns, who provided four generations of machine room wizards for the paper. It all began in 1903, when Mr Robert Talbot Lawn was recruited from the *Croydon Advertiser* in readiness for the *County Press* re-equipping with a Hoe Rotary Press. From then on the machine room was to be run by successive members of the family, until the paper closed its printing works in September, 1997, and had publication carried out under contract by *The News* at Hilsea, Portsmouth.

R T Lawn, Bob as he was universally known, had a distinctive waxed moustache giving him the appearance of a military man. And that was no false impression. He served in the Boer War and maintained his links with the army when he came to the Island, serving as a sergeant in the Territorial Army with the IW Rifles. In the First World War he was wounded in the epic action at Suvla Bay, where the Rifles sustained heavy losses when they took part in the ill-fated Gallipoli operations against the Turks.

Four of the five members of the Lawn family to work for the CP (from left), Alan; his father, Bob; grandfather, Bob, and uncle, Kenneth

While in hospital in Egypt Sgt Lawn's term of engagement ended and he was able to return to the *County Press* and relieve Mr George Brannon of his machine room duties. He continued as machine room foreman until going into semi-retirement in 1954, on completing just over 50 years, finally retiring five years later after a record of service that was certainly above the call of duty.

Bob's elder son, also named Robert Talbot and inevitably known as Young Bob, joined the *County Press* in 1923 as a 14-year-old. (His younger brother, Kenneth, also worked for the paper as a printer before taking up employment on the mainland). Young Bob had an early baptism of fire after his father's foot was crushed by a three-hundredweight roller in a machine room accident. When a request for volunteers to take over the stereotyping fell on deaf ears, Young Bob was asked if he would do it.

So he stepped into the breach and worked through the night processing the flongs on which the impression of pages were made before being cast into metal pages for attaching to the rotary printing press. The flongs were made from a combination of thick and thin blotting paper and tissue paper, mixed with flour and water and other ingredients to a secret recipe handed down to Young Bob by his father. The secret of the recipe lost its mystery with the introduction of purpose-made flongs.

Young Bob, who provided the author with invaluable reminiscences and material before his death, aged 88, in July, 1999, recalled that he received an extra three shillings and sixpence for this Herculean effort – the equivalent to 17.5p in today's money. He carried on doing the job each Friday night for 14 weeks until his father was fit enough to return to work. His reward, after his bosses overheard he was none too pleased with just a two-shilling a week bonus, was to have his seven-year apprenticeship reduced by a year.

Apprentices in his days started on four shillings a week for the first month, rising to five shillings for the rest of the year. Their pay then rose by two shillings and sixpence a week a year, so by the seventh and final year it had reached £1 a week. Those who showed great promise were rewarded by a big jump in wages to £3 a week for the final three months of their apprenticeship. Less fortunate, during the mass unemployment of the 1920s, were the men who, each Friday at midnight just before the presses rolled, would gather outside the works entrance in the hope of being among the half-dozen picked as casual labourers for a four-hour stint that would earn them five shillings.

For many years the firm printed guides for Carisbrooke Castle and Osborne House. Every Saturday morning during the summer three apprentices were given the task of delivering the castle guides in a handcart. The route grew progressively steeper up to the castle and the practice was to have two apprentices on ropes in front and one on the handles. Young Bob recalled a particularly eventful Saturday. "We were half-way up the hill when the lad on the handles had a sneezing fit. He let go, the cart upended and guides went all over the road."

Murphy's law was certainly at work that day because as Bob and his two colleagues feverishly collected the scattered parcels what should come down the hill but Princess Beatrice's car from the Island's royal Governor's official residence at the castle. Her chauffeur-driven Daimler came to a stately halt as the by now red-faced apprenticeship trio completed the retrieval of their guides. "The Princess was soon on her way and smiled and waved to us on passing," said Bob. "We feared for the worst when we got back, but nothing was said so no complaint had been made." From what I have heard from other Islanders who remember Princess Beatrice, it was typical of her kindly disposition that she would not want to get anyone into trouble for what after all was an accident.

World War II was as eventful for Young Bob as the First World War had been for his father. As a sergeant-major in the Royal Artillery he was in both of the momentous sieges at Tobruk, in North Africa, in 1942. The second one ended with him and his surviving comrades being captured by Field Marshal Rommel's forces. He was detailed to supervise a party of native workmen to clear up a hotel. It was to be Rommel's headquarters and when the job was finished the famous German commander came over to Sgt-Maj Lawn, shook his hand and said: "Sergento-maturo, your war is over."

During his three years as a prisoner-of-war his weight plummeted from 17 stones to just seven, on a 1,500-mile forced march as his German captors tried to evade Russians advancing from the east and Americans and British forces from the west. Of the 2,000 prisoners who started out, only 500 survived.

Young Bob, who regained his weightlifter physique, was not only a tower of strength to the *County Press*, but was also a bastion of the Ancient Order of Foresters in which he held many senior positions. Just as he succeeded his father as machine room foreman, so he in turn handed over to his son, Alan, on retirement in 1975 after 52 years' magnificent service. To that can be added the couple or so years he did as a *County Press* paperboy from the age of 11, getting up at 5.30am to deliver 25 dozen copies each Saturday on an extensive, not to say exhausting, round in Newport. He showed an entrepreneurial approach by adding to his one shilling a week pay by buying an extra couple of dozen papers at trade price (one-and-a-half old pennies) and reselling at half-a-penny profit to men as they arrived for work at the Quay at 6am.

Alan, who helped oversee the transfer of printing to the Riverway Industrial Estate at Newport in 1985, was joined by his son, Mark, who had started his career in 1979 at Saunders, the Shanklin printers which formerly published the *IW Guardian* and later the merged *IW Chronicle-Guardian*. The *County Press* bought Saunders in 1978 and closed it two years later because it was losing money. When the Riverway Works was closed, Alan retired after 44 years of carrying on the Lawn tradition at the *County Press*.

In December, 1987, he had made the headlines himself when a joke backfired, forcing him to jump fully clothed into the icy waters of the River Medina. He made the big splash after telling workmates he would jump into the river at high tide if they could raise £100 for the Children In Need Appeal within an hour. They took up the challenge and raised £175, leaving Alan for the high jump!

Footnote: Mark Lawn was one of two employees from the paper to fill jobs in The News' machine room at Hilsea. So the family's remarkable record in the print continues. ◆

CHAPTER SEVEN **ELECTION SHOWCASE**

Once again I delved into the memory bank of Mr Bob Lawn junior for an insight into what happened at General Elections in the days before there were regular news bulletins on the wireless.

The Newspaper Society sent daily telegrams to the *County Press* to keep it abreast of national and international events. As well as the information being included in the paper, the telegrams were posted in the front office windows. At times staff could not see out because there were so many. Passers-by used to stop to read them and the window gazing reached intense proportions at elections as Islanders crowded around the *County Press* version of Peter Snow's swingometer.

Mr Lawn recalled: "Eleven o'clock those nights, the *County Press* rushed to prepare for the results as they came through to be written out and posted in the window. Usually by 11.30 the first results were through and posted and then the crowds gathered in the High Street and waited for the rest. We had telephones on the go the whole night, with 30 of us keeping the news going and posted. It certainly was hectic. All the rooms were in operation and gallons of tea and coffee were continually being provided.

"By midnight the High Street was packed solid with people from the *County Press* windows right across the road to under the arches of the Guildhall. These crowds continued the whole night through and some scuffles ensued as Conservative, Liberal and Labour could never agree. It all added to the spice and excitement of days long ago. We went home for breakfast at eight o'clock when the day shift started and replaced us. Then it was back to our normal work an hour later."

Bob added: "I believe it was in 1945 that I was sent down to the County Hall to verify the Island result – the runner having returned to say that the Conservatives had again won the Island but with a very small majority, which was not believed by the higher-ups at the office. I came back and confirmed that the runner was right."

For the record, Bob's memory had not failed him. It was in 1945, when Labour scored a shock national landslide, that Canadian-born Capt Peter Macdonald retained the seat for the Conservatives with a majority of 2,784 over the Labour candidate, Col W J Miller. The Liberal candidate, a long way behind in third place, was Miss May O'Connor, who gave outstanding service to the Island as chairman of the county education committee.

Alderman Mark Woodnutt

In 1945, his 21st year as an MP, Capt Macdonald was knighted. He had represented the Island from 1924, when he wrested it from the Liberals, and held the seat – winning no fewer than eight elections – until announcing his retirement in 1958. He was succeeded by the late Ald Mark Woodnutt, who continued the Conservative's supremacy on the Island until being sensationally defeated in 1974. Liberal Mr Stephen Ross, later Lord Ross, wiped out a Conservative majority of more than 17,000 in polling nearly 8,000 more votes than Ald Woodnutt.

Four year earlier, the 1970 contest had seen the fledgling Vectis Nationalist Party field its

general secretary, Mr Ronald Cawdell, as its candidate. He came fourth with 1,607 votes. Mr Cawdell, a member of Ryde Borough Council and the county council, formed the VNP primarily as part of the campaign for the Island to retain its independent county status, which was successfully accomplished two years later.

Stephen Ross held the seat for 13 years until retiring on health grounds before the 1987 election. His closest electoral call came in 1979 when he defeated the Conservative challenger, Mr Dudley Fishburn, by 352 votes after a recount. Lord Ross died in 1993, aged 66. Mr Barry Field returned the Island to the Tory fold in 1987, a feat that in 1983 had proved beyond Mrs Virginia Bottomley, who later became a high-flying member of the Cabinet. Mr Field had a 6,442 margin over Mr Michael Young for the Liberal-Alliance, with Mr Kenn Pearson polling 4,626 for Labour.

Mr Field saw his majority cut to 1,827 five years later when he held off Dr Peter Brand of the Liberal Democrats, a cliff-hanger result very much in line with an Islandwide opinion poll conducted by the *County Press*. The demanding task of representing the Island, the largest seat in the country in terms of voters on the register, took its toll of even Mr Field's robust health and he stood down due to a stress-related illness, aged 50, in January, 1997.

His successor as Tory candidate, Mr Andrew Turner, had only a matter of weeks before Prime Minister John Major called the election for May 1 and he lost to Dr Brand by 6,406 votes. New Labour, led by Mr Tony Blair, swept to victory nationally with a mammoth majority. It could also take some comfort from the Island result, with Mrs Deborah Gardiner doubling the party's 1992 vote of 4,784. The local contest saw a record line-up in modern times of nine candidates. ◆

CHAPTER EIGHT **TRAINING GROUND**

As a training ground for reporters the *County Press* has a proven record in providing recruits for Fleet Street and latterly that new home for some national newspapers, Docklands. At the time of going to press Richard Orchard, from Freshwater, was on the *Sun*; David Leigh, from Liphook, Hants, was with the *Daily Mirror* and Heather Mills was social affairs editor for the *Observer*.

Heather, who has returned to live on the Island, began her Fleet Street career at the Press Association and then moved to the *Daily Telegraph* before becoming one of the original members of the *Independent's* editorial team.

Patrick Davis, from an older generation of *County Press* reporters, edited the *IW Times* for a period in the 1950s before launching into a highly successful career on the mainland which took him to the *Yorkshire Evening Post* and London's *Evening Standard*. This led to the *Times*, where he held a series of senior positions including deputy foreign news editor, joint assistant managing editor in charge of the editorial management unit and foreign manager. He had been living at Yarmouth for about four years before his death in July, 1998, aged 70.

Vicki Couchman, who cut her photographic teeth as a trainee on the *County Press*, is a photo-journalist with a flair for creativity and adventure, now running a travel publishing company at Portsmouth called Travellerseye. She has published two acclaimed books on her travels in the Far East and South America, where her willingness to go native has rewarded her with evocative photographs denied to colleagues who keep to the beaten track. In 1998 Vicki, whose parents live in Whitwell, won a £1,000 prize in an *Independent on Sunday* picture competition and more recently she has been getting national exposure in the *Sunday Times' Style* magazine.

Continuing on this trail of success of ex-*County Press* staff, listeners to Radio 4 may be familiar with the name and voice of Rebecca Carr, while anyone who has explored the web site pages of the *Financial Times* could well have read the input of Catherine Kelly.

I salute them all and hasten to add that not all the best journalists work for the national media, with the present *County Press* editorial team providing ample proof that there is plenty of talent in the provinces. Former *County Press* sports editor Keith Newbery is a classic example of this. The editorial mastermind of the early successes of the *IW Weekly Post*, Keith became an award-winning columnist with *The News* at Portsmouth, headhunted by more than one national newspaper which recognised an outstanding talent. His love of the Isle of Wight was probably the main reason he rejected such overtures. He is now executive editor of a group of weekly papers in Chichester, but still lives at Winford, near Newchurch.

My vote for the *County Press* Reporter of the Era goes to Roy Blackman. He joined the paper as a 16-year-old from Ryde School and in choosing him for this accolade I may be accused of bias. This is because, having become a junior reporter a few months before Roy in 1950 and having introduced him to the intricacies of making the office tea, I have followed his career with great interest, not to say envy.

But let the record speak for itself. Roy came under the tutelage of Gerry Roberts, who ran the Ryde office and whose premature death in 1961, aged 53, unquestionably robbed the *County Press* of a future editor. Roy told me that he counted himself extremely fortunate to learn the trade from Gerry Roberts, whose wife, Win, worked at head office before becoming the long-serving Bembridge correspondent for the paper. It was at Ryde that Roy worked with another highly respected reporter, the softly spoken Fred Kingswell and someone much nearer his own age, the pretty Rosemary Crimp, who married an army officer.

Roy's introduction to journalism was sidetracked for a few months when he was seconded to fill a temporary vacancy in the readers' room. To this day he recalls with horror how he spent hour after hour in a attic cubby-hole of an

Roy Blackman at a news conference in Moscow

office reading every name in the Island telephone directory published by the *County Press* and painstakingly checking an endless list of figures for a seismology magazine. Two years National Service proved an unexpected turning point in Roy's career. After starting out in the infantry he was transferred to the Intelligence Corps where he learned Russian at the height of the Cold War in East-West relations.

In 1955 he joined the Portsmouth *Evening News* based at Cowes, but his knowledge of Russian saw him called to head office to help with coverage of the visit to Britain of Kremlin leaders Bulganin and Khruschev. They had arrived in Portsmouth aboard the heavy cruiser *Ordzhonikidze* and a major diplomatic row broke out when the Russians accused British intelligence of using a frogman to spy on the ship.

This became known as the Buster Crabbe affair because it was alleged that the frogman was Cmdr Buster Crabbe, whose disappearance gave rise to speculation that he had been abducted or killed by the Russians. Roy recalls scouring hotel registers in Portsmouth and Southsea in the hunt to establish that Cmdr Crabbe had stayed locally before the incident. A headless body washed up a year later was believed to be that of the missing officer.

From *The News* Roy joined the *Daily Mirror*, working first on its diary page and then as a feature writer. He graduated to defence correspondent and reported from trouble spots around the world, including the Indian-Pakistan border war and upheavals in Indonesia and Africa. He was arrested several times and spent some uncomfortable days in jails where all mod cons were sadly lacking.

It was while reporting on the Vietnam War that he was headhunted by the *Daily Express*, with the promise of becoming Moscow correspondent in a short time. Roy's finest journalistic hour came in the Russian capital when he obtained a world scoop – the first interview with the spy Kim Philby since he fled to Russia from the Lebanon as the British security services were closing in.

Philby, who at the time of his defection was the Middle East correspondent for a Sunday newspaper, was notorious as the Third Man linked to those other traitors, Burgess and Maclean. Like Philby, they were senior officers in the KGB, the Russian secret service. Roy approached a senior KGB representative and discussed the possibilities of interviewing Philby. I still have a mind's-eye picture of my erstwhile colleague being interviewed on *Panorama* about his big scoop.

Roy said he regarded his two-and-a-half years in Russia in the late 1960s, which also encompassed the Soviet invasion of Czechoslovakia, as a very exciting and rewarding time. Even then he said it was possible to see that the beginning of the end of Communism was underway and that its downfall would come from within because of the crippling impact on the economy of trying to compete with the Americans militarily.

Two years in Paris followed, with the death of General de Gaulle the most important event during that time. On returning to London he was House of Commons lobby correspondent for the *Express* from 1971 to '76. This was a gruelling assignment, working against tight deadlines and for very long hours.

Not surprisingly, Roy eventually decided to retire from journalism and tried farming in Sussex. Financially that was not a very profitable experience and in 1980 he started a new career in public relations in the City. His speciality has been advising on Press strategy in major take-over bids, mostly being involved with companies resisting such moves – his Fleet Street know-how proving invaluable in the 35 City battles he has been engaged in.

When I last spoke to Roy he was contemplating partial retirement after a working life he could never have imagined would be so eventful when he started out as junior reporter for the *County Press*. ◆

CHAPTER NINE **ON THE SOCIAL SIDE**

For those of us for whom the social side of the *County Press* nowadays is confined to a pre-Christmas meal with our colleagues at a pub or restaurant it is a revelation to learn of what used to happen in the inter-war years. My informant, as on other aspects of the paper's history, was Mr Bob Lawn junior.

One of the highlights of the year for the staff, which continued to my knowledge for a number of years after the Second World War, was the annual Wayzgoose – the peculiar name for a printers' outing. Mr Lawn had traced the origins of Wayzgoose which he found in *Moxon's Mechanic Exercises*, the first English book on printing, published in 1683. The name is derived from the era when each year the master printer gave his journeymen a Waygoose – a good feast, which he held at his home – and also provided money to spend at the ale house or tavern at night.

Traditionally, the *County Press* Wayzgoose was held on the first Monday in July and invariably involved a day's outing to a county cricket match, a visit to a paper mill, or a charabanc trip to a seaside town or through the New Forest. Management always made sure there was plenty to eat and drink and it was a cheerful, if tired, party that returned to the Island after the day out.

During August Mr George Brannon, the Old Governor as Mr Lawn affectionately called him, arranged for everyone to leave work one Monday morning at 11.30am to go to a garden party at his Carisbrooke home, Clatterford House. "Various games and competitions were held and a concert party came to entertain us from either Sandown or Shanklin pier," Mr Lawn recalled. "Cakes, sandwiches and plenty of liquid refreshments were available the whole time and it was known for the Governor to ask us at 11pm to make certain all was drunk-up before we went home as he only wanted empties to go back."

George Brannon outside Clatterford House, Carisbrooke

The last Friday in November, when the company celebrated its anniversary, was another red-letter day. It was then that meat pies, mince pies and drinks were laid on, with more than enough left over for those printing the paper overnight.

During the early 1920s the *County Press* formed a social club, each member paying sixpence a week for expenses. During the summer months there were outings on Saturday to the seaside. Mr Lawn said he well remembered going to Puckaster Cove, near Niton, for swimming, with tea afterwards at the Buddle Inn. Brighstone Beach with tea taken in the New Inn, swimming at Brook and then tea in one of the houses on the green. Gurnard and Colwell Bay were also on the summer itinerary.

When the strawberry season was at its height, boats used to come across the Solent from Southampton to the Folly Inn on the River Medina laden with the fruit, to be served at special strawberry and cream teas. These were a 'must' for social club members at least twice a summer and they would return home with wooden baskets piled with two-and-a-half-pounds of strawberries costing one shilling (5p).

In the winter whist drives were held in the machine room and the big night of the year was New Year's Eve when club members and their wives danced till late in the machine room, while whist drives were held in the news and jobbing rooms. Food and drink were plentiful and on the stroke of midnight a steaming bowl of potent punch was brought over from Warburton's Hotel and placed on the flong-making trolley, from where it was handed round during the singing of *Auld Lang Syne*.

The festivities carried on until the early hours although, Mr Lawn said, the directors usually left the party at 1.30am. "Getting home was the trouble," he remembered. "On one occasion six members of the staff had seen each other home and all finished up back at the *County Press*, so they decided to stay there for what was left of the night."

That first social club became an unexpected victim of the General Strike of 1926. The secretary of the club, who also happened to be secretary of the works committee of the main printing union, the Typographical Society, did not join the strike, although he had signed the telegrams informing his members of strike action. The six apprentices, who were not allowed to join the strike, sent the "blackleg" to Coventry as did his colleagues when they returned to work.

Members of the *County Press* on a 'Wayzgoose' to Morris Motors, Cowley, in 1938

After the demise of the social club the apprentices, with some of the younger men, formed the Icke Club – there is no particular significance in the name, it was just that it was different!

The Ickes bought an ex-army bell tent, a primus stove and other equipment needed for the outdoor life and had camping weekends at Brighstone Grange between Easter and September. During the winter they used to cycle out to places like Gurnard for tea, paid for out of club funds which also covered a packet of Players' cigarettes each. Later the Ickes had a table tennis table made and this was set up on the upper floor of the *County Press* building next to the binding room. At the beginning of the Second World War this table was given to one of the drill halls at Newport for the use of the troops visiting the canteen run by the WVS (now the WRVS).

Entering floats in carnivals was another activity on the crowded staff social scene of those days, when making one's own entertainment was a way of life. Over the years the social club has sprung back into life for a time, holding dinners and arranging trips and treats for the children of staff, though latterly it has fallen into the doldrums. Perhaps this account of what used to happen might spark another revival. ◆

Six former employees, who together gave more than 320 years service to the company, are included in this centenary year photograph of CP staff and directors. They are all in the third row from the front.

Leslie Rodaway is on the right of editor Stephen Rea, while the other five are at the opposite end of the row (from the left), Percy Appel, Jack Coombes, Bob Lawn, Roy Hannam and Tom Saunders

CHAPTER TEN **THE CHARACTERS**

Every company has them. Those members of staff whom everyone seems to know, from the boss to the cleaners. They are Characters with a capital C. Perhaps it is because of a cheeky turn of phrase, a twinkle in the eye, or the way they wear their hair – short or long, there are usually no half-measures for them – or perhaps they have a big personality that makes them natural charmers.

Whatever it is, one commodity they usually have in common is plenty of self-confidence. Not for them the Yes Sir, No Sir, approach to life. They speak their mind and you either admire them or not for that.

In choosing the Characters for this book I have confined myself to those I have known personally and, as that spans only just under a half-a-century of experience, I must apologise to those before my time.

I will start with the late Harold Minns, a dark, balding man with thick horn-rimmed glasses, a loud but friendly voice and a liking, or should I say an addiction, to strong tobacco which he rolled into cigarettes himself. He succeeded his father as the *County Press*'s Cowes reporter. Covering yachting was one of his main activities in the summer and Harold had the distinction in the decade or so after the Second World War of being the only reporter, local or national, to be allowed into the hallowed portals of the Royal Yacht Squadron, the world's most elite yacht club.

Actually I think he was permitted simply to go into the signalman's hut to get race results but that was farther than any other reporter reached and was enough in itself to put Harold in a class of his own. After each Cowes Week he used to spend his own relaxing week in Brighton, an expedition that always produced something out of the ordinary, such as the time he came back and said he had stumbled across a party where all the men were dressed as women and vice versa – not, I hasten to add, that macho Harold would have worn anything but his standard navy blue blazer and grey flannels.

A contemporary of Harold's was Bob Clegg, who cut his journalistic teeth in his native Yorkshire. He was ex-RAF with a liking for a flutter and I well remember him phoning his bookie under the pseudonym of Bob Albion – the Albion in this case being the Albion Hotel at Freshwater Bay, one of Bob's favourite calls for a drink as he covered the West Wight district from his Freshwater home.

He was a superb all-rounder, equally capable at reporting parish councils as compiling graphic accounts of rescue missions by Yarmouth lifeboat. One of the latter won him an award from the RNLI for the best factual account of a lifeboat rescue in 1966. Sadly, Bob died the following year, aged 53.

Morris Barton

But it was his freelancing activities for which I will best remember Bob. At first glance the sparsely populated West Wight does not appear a very fertile ground for news, but 'Clegg, Freshwater', was a familiar name to Fleet Street copytakers as he filed story after story. It was extraordinary how often the first cuckoo of the year was heard in West Wight

and if you became trapped on a cliff in the area you could rest assured that your escapade would find its way into the national newspapers.

Of course the reporting staff does not have a monopoly on Characters. Far from it. After all, printers are in a class of their own when it comes to speaking their minds and Morris Barton and Jeff Manners, who both took early retirement, are cases in point. They benefited during their employment from the encouragement the company gave to staff to take part in public life.

Morris, a politician to his fingertips, was leader of the IW County Council and its successor unitary authority for 15 years. He was employed by the company for nearly 40 years and was newsroom overseer before becoming head reader for the last 20 years. His activities at County Hall and elsewhere took up more column inches in the *County Press* than anyone else's. This led to some accusations that he wrote or vetted his own reports; but nothing could have been further from the truth and it defies belief that he would have written the critical reports that not infrequently appeared about him. These often spurred him into writing to the editor and getting additional space on the letters pages. At least he could save on postage . . .

Morris and Jeff, although work colleagues and sometimes political allies, have had a rather up and down relationship in the corridors of power and they could not be more unlike physically. Morris, tall and dark – Jeff rotund and redfaced with a white cap of hair. Jeff, a one-time father of the chapel, has a reputation as a rebel at County Hall, with the knack of beating all who try to deprive him of his Parkhurst seat. He makes a joke of his right-wing leanings despite his Liberal label and often throws caution to the wind when he mounts his characteristic verbal assaults which have made many headlines.

Jeff Manners

He started up a security business while still on the *County Press*, where he worked in several capacities, latterly as a keyboard operator, and so a job was waiting for him when he retired.

That *County Press* giant, the late Bob Lawn, junior, obviously warrants inclusion in this list but I have already put my readers in the picture about Bob.

Back to the reporting scene – and no round-up of Characters could exclude Lewis Grant. He was the last district reporter on the paper after the others were centralised at head office as improved communications made it unnecessary to have staff spread around the Island.

Lew, as he is known to colleagues and friends, has never lost his Scottish burr despite having lived on the Island for 50 years. He used to file copy to the *County Press* long before joining it, under a contract for coverage of the Sandown and Shanklin area with the *IW Chronicle* for which he worked for many years.

His output was prodigious, as was his devotion to duty. While most reporters these days would understandably feel hard done by if asked to cover more than two evening jobs a week – they get no overtime, after all – Lew hardly had a night at home. I remember once meeting him as he was off to yet another evening engagement: the 11th in a fortnight. But for all the stress of the job I never knew him to be anything but cheerful. Lew is a man of great humanity, who, with his wife, Betty, used to give holidays to under-privileged children from a Europe still recovering from war. Finally retiring for a well earned rest in 1990, he still contributes stories to the paper and it was no surprise when in 1996 he was one of those chosen to receive a certificate honouring men and women who had worked hard for the Shanklin, Lake and Sandown communities.

Now to someone who has been the rock of successive editorial teams since he rejoined the *County Press* in the mid-1970s, having had a brief earlier spell on the paper ten years earlier. In turn assistant editor, associate editor and for the last 11 years deputy editor, Yorkshireman Mike Sutcliffe is a man of many talents. As well as being a consummate journalist, combining an eye for detail with a flair for creative page make-up, he is a dedicated professional respected by management and popular with staff.

He is a prankster – whether compiling a fictitious letter of complaint to put the wind-up some unsuspecting colleague or affecting his mimic's voice in making an equally mischievous phone call.

Mike is the darling of the WIs and Townswomen's Guilds on the Island for his wit and humour at the annual presentations of *County Press* trophies to their correspondents of the year; while his expertise on the piano keep him in demand as an accompanist to one of the Island's best known groups of amateur entertainers.

Current deputy chief reporter Gavin Foster has not only made headlines in the national press – he's even been the subject of an advertising campaign on Southern Vectis buses. Gavin first shot to prominence in 1991 when, as a passionate fan of West Ham United FC and the Rolling Stones, he had his name changed to Gavin West Ham United Football Club The Boleyn Ground Upton Park EC 13 I'm Forever Blowing Bubbles The Rolling Stones Mick and Keith God Bless The Midnight Ramblers Foster.

Ostensibly he changed to this mind-boggling nomenclature to raise money for charity and certainly that is where all the payments he received from the national newspapers went. But under the heading of Now It Can Be Told I can exclusively reveal that Gavin was not as altruistic as he seemed at the time.

Gavin Foster

It was simply that he was broke and wanted to earn extra cash, but having been found breaking a cardinal law by giving another paper a story before it had appeared in the *County Press* – in this case his renaming ceremony – he had no option but to make his generous donation.

His bus publicity came in the wake of having his trademark shoulder-length hair cut to a virtually short back and sides. Realising the Island-shaking implications, Southern Vectis group managing director Stuart Lynn hastily arranged a series of posters on the back of buses to the effect, "We're not sure about Gavin's new haircut. What do you think!"

Bless you, Gavin. We need Characters like you and the colleagues I have mentioned to brighten up our own mundane lives. ◆

CHAPTER ELEVEN **A NEW HOME**

The official opening of Brannon House as the modern new home of the *County Press* on the site of the former printing works in Pyle Street will go down as one of the most memorable days in the history of the company. Although its pages had played host to royalty from virtually the paper's first edition, it had not been honoured before by the presence of a member of the Royal Family in person.

Small wonder then that a special supplement was published in May 1992 to mark the day when the Duke of York declared the splendid new building open; incidentally, there are no prizes for guessing why its name was chosen! There was no doubt that his Royal Highness was determined to enjoy his day trip to the Island. As a Royal Navy helicopter pilot he had been on dangerous operations during the Falklands War in 1982, but it was very much a peaceful and pleasurable mission when he flew a red helicopter from the Queen's Flight to the Island on May 22.

At the *County Press*, reporters accustomed to asking the questions had the tables turned on them when the Duke took an impromptu walkabout around their desks. As one who had often been hounded by the Press he seemed to enjoy the opportunity to have journalists on the receiving end. He chatted to features editor Ron Kentish on the electronic advances made in newspaper production, spoke to sports editor John Hamon about the former Royal IW Golf Club at St Helens and quizzed deputy editor Mike Sutcliffe about his work.

Among the reporters he questioned was Rachael Rosewell, now a sub-editor. When she told the Duke she had spent the morning covering court cases, he asked her why newspapers

Brannon House, Pyle
Street, Newport

seemed to concentrate on bad news. Rachael was up to the challenge, telling the Duke that the *County Press* published far more good news than bad and was looking forward to covering his visit.

Before the opening ceremony the then editor, Peter Hurst, took the Duke on a tour of the editorial department and works director Tony Thorpe showed him the typesetting, proof-reading and paste-up sections. In the advertising department he met advertising manager Alistair Porteous and his staff.

On his arrival at the *County Press* the Duke had been welcomed by the company chairman, Mr Richard Bradbeer, who presented his wife, Rosemary, managing director Robin Freeman and other members of the board, Mr Charles Bullworthy, Mr David Cheverton, Mr Mark Hammer and Mrs Marilyn Lawson.

During his tour of Brannon House, which had been occupied since the move from the High Street premises the previous October, the Duke saw articles from January, 1901, reporting the death at Osborne House of his great-great-great-grandmother, Queen Victoria. The royal visitor and his entourage, including the Island's Governor, Lord Mottistone, joined guests in a marquee erected on the Brannon House car park.

There he met the architects and representatives of the builders of the £1 million-plus building and was invited by Mr Bradbeer to unveil a commemorative plaque. "Next week we will be able to report ourselves," said Mr Bradbeer, who presented the Duke with an engraving of Osborne House by Alfred Brannon, father of the *County Press* co-founder.

After chatting with employees from the accounts and printing departments, the Duke was whisked off to Wroxall Primary School to perform a commemoration ceremony marking the birth of the new school building, opened in 1986 at a cost of £500,000. His final engagement of the day was to open the new £325,000 modern languages block at Ryde School.

At each stop on his itinerary the Duke found long-serving *County Press* employee Mr Keith Lacey, overseer in the camera and platemaking department, among those waiting to greet him. As county council chairman, Mr Lacey, with his wife, Pat, an ex-*County Press* employee herself, had to be there ahead of the royal guest. Keeping out in front was not easy. Nothing was allowed to delay the royal timetable – not even traffic lights showing red at the notorious Coppins Bridge bottleneck in Newport, where police officers waved back other traffic.

The Duke was warmly received by crowds of well-wishers wherever he went and his visit provided a field day for *County Press* chief photographer Chris Thwaites and colleagues Peter Boam, Vivienne Ventress and Ian Pert who took the pictures for the special supplement.

Space and Style for the 21st Century was the headline over a scene-setting article by Ron Kentish in praise of Brannon House, built by Geoffrey Osborne, Ltd, of Newport. "Step inside and you will immediately be aware of the sense of space, style and distinctive architectural touches that are a feature of the whole building," he wrote. "If the former High Street offices represented some of the finest examples of late Victorian architecture, then Brannon House will be seen in a hundred years time as worthy of the same regard.

"The heavy mahogany panelling so carefully restored and renovated at 29 High Street remains a classic example of its period. In its place in the new building are a number of natural ash features, including the main counter, screens and elegant, sweeping spiral staircase. This, together with the terrazzo floor finish and feature lighting, creates an impressive welcome to Brannon House, built for the 21st century."

Mr Freeman said the architects, A G Biggs Partnership, responsible for the design work, translated precisely what the management was trying to achieve. "We wanted something that was curved, had no hard edges and was both welcoming and easy on the eye. We believe that has been achieved, while at the same time maintaining our own distinctive image – that of a long-established newspaper which is very much a part of the community ."

Behind the spacious reception area and counter, the ground floor accommodates the advertising and marketing department. The main reception area also leads via the spiral staircase to the first floor open-plan space housing the editorial and production departments.

In contrast to the open-plan look of the first floor, the second floor consists of a number of offices, including those for senior management and finance, the boardroom, photographic platemaking workshops and staff room and kitchenette.

Frankly, the whole environment of Brannon House could not have been more removed from the rabbit warren of offices and rooms that were a feature of 29 High Street behind the mahogany splendour of the front office. For all that the old building had served the company well for 80 years as it was repeatedly altered internally to accommodate the changing demands of the business and staff.

Ten years after taking over the editorial chair, Peter Hurst took early retirement on health grounds, aged 58, in December, 1997. The outstanding success of the MRI appeal is a lasting legacy of his leadership and he also had the satisfaction of knowing that he left the paper in prime condition, with sales heading for 38,000 a week in the peak summer months.

The new editor, Gosport-born Brian Dennis, 46, had a hat-trick of editorships under his belt in the Midlands, Cumbria and Scotland. He has already taken several initiatives to develop the paper's involvement in the community, such as the toy appeal, the introduction of awards for amateur theatre company productions and giving greater impetus to the Village Ventures awards scheme. Mr Dennis was appointed a director in August 1999.

Sales reached a record 40,610 weekly average that month and the results of a survey of Islanders published in September enabled the paper to proudly claim that it was the most popular local weekly newspaper in the country. The survey, by specialist media research company RSGB, showed that 94 percent of Islanders above the age of 15 read the paper in an average month and that the majority of Islanders saw the *County Press* as their principal source of local news.

This all bore out what Mr Dennis said when he succeeded Peter Hurst: "I regard the *County Press* as one of the best local newspapers anywhere in the country. It is packed with news, views, sport and information – a paper of integrity which can properly claim to be the Voice of the Island." ◆

CHAPTER TWELVE **DOWN THE DECADES –
A LIVING HISTORY**

Isle of
Wight
County
Press

For 116 years the *County Press* has been the eyes and ears of the Island, keeping readers in touch with events, large and small, within the well-defined boundaries of its circulation area.

As has already been noted, for part of that time it also kept Islanders abreast of national and international news, but, in this necessarily subjective trip down memory lane, I have concentrated on Island news or events abroad affecting Islanders. Stories involving royal occasions have been dealt with in an earlier chapter.

It has been an exercise underlining the fact that in many cases there is nothing new under the sun as topics keep recurring, like a proposed link across or under the Solent, the state of the roads, unemployment, problems for farmers and the heroism of Island lifeboat crews.

1884 – 1900

The decade-and-a-half leading to the end of the century were highly newsworthy as the Island tasted tragedy and triumph, happiness and sadness.

There was certainly a mixture of all of these in 1888. Two members of the Brighstone lifeboat and one from the Brook lifeboat lost their lives while going to the aid of the 1,598-ton *Sirenia*, with a cargo of wheat from San Francisco, which foundered on Atherfield Ledge during thick fog on March 10.

After rescuing the captain's wife, three children and two of a crew of 26, the Brighstone boat returned to the wrecked vessel in rough weather between 1am and 2am and had taken off 13 of the crew when she was capsized by a tremendous wave.

When the lifeboat righted herself 22 of the 26 men who had been thrown into the raging water regained their places, but the gallant lifeboat coxswain, Moses Munt, and his equally brave assistant, Thomas Cotton, were drowned, with two of the *Sirenia*'s sailors. As the Brook lifeboat approached the doomed *Sirenia*, three of her crew were washed overboard and one of them, second coxswain Rufus Cooper, perished.

From sadness to happiness – that same year Ryde became the cradle of carnivals in this country by holding its first parade. Until then fairs and regattas were the major attractions but the Victorians craved something more as the Island developed as a holiday resort. So carnival English-style was born, with Ryde gaining royal approval in 1889 when Queen Victoria watched the parade from a horse-drawn carriage by the town hall.

Little wonder that in the same year Ventnor launched its carnival, another sign of the town's growing importance as 1887 had seen the opening of the Royal Victoria Pier.

An Edison phonograph, forerunner of the gramophone, stereo and the CD-player, was demonstrated at Ryde Theatre to an "amused and amazed" capacity audience in 1889, while the following year saw the first councillors elected for the newly created IW County Council and the formation of the Island's first independent county police force – 47 strong, under Supt J Duke.

The lifeboatmen of Atherfield, Brook and Brighstone won international fame for saving the 400 passengers and crew from the North German Lloyd liner *Eider*, after she became stranded on the treacherous Atherfield Ledge in February, 1892.

Queen Victoria led the mourning in October that year for her poet laureate, Alfred, Lord Tennyson, who died at his residence in Haslemere, Surrey. He had celebrated his 83rd birthday the previous August at Farringford, his Island home for 40 years. He succeeded Wordsworth in 1850 as poet laureate and five years later was raised to the peerage by a grateful monarch as Baron Tennyson of Aldworth (Surrey) and Freshwater.

The weather played havoc in 1893 with a serious drought in May, heavy thunderstorms in the late summer and severe gales in the autumn. The following January heavy snow heralded an intensely cold spell with 22.5 degrees of frost, leading to the River Medina freezing. People were able to walk and skate across up to a mile downstream of Newport.

The Island's knack of capturing attention showed itself again in December, 1897, when Guglielmo Marconi set up the world's first commercial radio transmitting station on a cliff-top site at Alum Bay. From the Needles Wireless Telegraph Station, this Italian genius of the airwaves began exchanging radio messages, first with a tug in Alum Bay, then with Bournemouth and Poole and later with ships 40 miles away.

One of those to assist him was the Totland postmaster, Mr J B Garlick, who had mastered Morse code.

Alfred, Lord Tennyson

Marconi had come to this country to try to interest the Post Office and the Royal Navy in his pioneering work with radio. He chose the Island as a base because of its accessibility to Portsmouth and Southampton and its relative freedom from electrical interference which was already proving a problem in urban areas.

While at Alum Bay he arranged a radio link-up between a cottage in the grounds of Osborne House and the Royal Yacht in Osborne Bay – an event commemorated at Osborne on the centenary by Marconi's daughter, Princess Eletra Marconi. This was largely due to the initiative of Island amateur radio enthusiasts who annually mark Marconi Day – the anniversary of his birth – with special transmissions.

Having sent the first paid-for radio telegram on June 3, 1898, the Needles station set another milestone on November 15, 1899, when it transmitted information for the first newspaper produced at sea – the *Transatlantic Times*, printed on the US liner *St Paul* when 36 miles off the Island. In 1900 the transmitter station at Alum Bay was moved to Knowles Farm, Niton, the forerunner of the modern Niton Radio.

The final year of the old century found Britain at war with the Boers – Dutch settlers – in South Africa. The first troops from the Island to be caught up in the conflict were regulars from Parkhurst Barracks, the 1st Battalion of the Rifle Brigade. They took part in the desperate fighting leading to the relief of Ladysmith and suffered heavy casualties.

Many Island men were among the reservists who went on active service before the war's end in 1902 and an Island contingent of volunteers, led by Captain Jack Seely, was among the first contingent of the Imperial Yeomanry which sailed from Southampton for South Africa.

Other volunteers, from the Princess Beatrice's IW Rifles, also responded promptly to the call to arms. Before their departure they were inspected in the grounds of Osborne House by Princess Beatrice, watched by Queen Victoria. There were a number of Islanders too in an active service section of the Hants and IW Artillery Militia who saw service in the war.

The Yeomanry, gallantly led by Capt Seely who was awarded the DSO, suffered the most casualties but fortunately the losses overall among the Islanders were not too severe, although disease as well as gunfire did claim some lives.

Locally, the *County Press* reported the death on May 11, 1898, of Mr Alexander Dabell, aged 90, proprietor of Blackgang Chine, who took a leading role in the development of Blackgang where he had settled 50 years before. He started the first seaside bazaars – the gift shops of their day – in the Island at Ryde, Shanklin, Ventnor and Blackgang.

Also in 1898 the Island telephone system of the National Telephone Co was completed in the summer when the line to Freshwater was opened. The principal Island town authorities consented to the local Electricity Company's application for a provisional order empowering the installation of electric light.

May the following year saw the completion of the Ocean Hotel, Sandown, described as one of the finest establishments of its kind on the South Coast. In the sporting field there was less to celebrate. Cowes Football Club's ambitious decision to field a professional side in the Southern League came to a premature end in its first season in 1899. After winning only two of the first 13 matches the team was withdrawn from the competition at Christmas.

1900 – 1910

There was a comforting start to the new century for members of the Royal IW Agricultural Society when an improved financial position was reported at the annual meeting. Ryde Corporation was in a contented mood as well, as members accepted Miss Brigstocke's offer to purchase the recreation ground and give it to the town – "this being only one of the many benefactions of this esteemed friend of Ryde".

The Cowes to Ventnor direct railway service was made possible by the completion of the line from St Lawrence to the Ventnor West terminus.

Sir Richard Webster, QC, retired as the Island's MP on his appointment as Master of the Rolls and elevation to the peerage as Lord Alverstone. Later in 1900 he became Lord Chief Justice.

War hero Capt Seely, destined to become a general and a peer, retained the seat for the Conservatives at the May by-election while still serving in South Africa. In his absence his attractive wife took to the hustings and helped him achieve a record majority of 1,262 over Mr, later Sir, Godfrey Baring – himself at the start of a record-breaking 51-year stint as chairman of the IW County Council, lasting until 1949. Capt Seely was re-elected unopposed at the so-called khaki election in October, 1900.

The County Asylum Committee was strongly criticised because the weekly charge for pauper patients was 11s 1d per head (just over 55p), compared with 8s 9d at the Hampshire Asylum.

Public meetings at Cowes and East Cowes ratified the decision of the two district councils to promote a Parliamentary Bill to acquire the ferry rights at Cowes on the expiration of the lease of the Southampton and IW Steampacket Co.

Complaints by cyclists' organisations of thorny hedge trimmings left on the road and puncturing riders' new pneumatic tyres led to the fining of a West Wight farmer, while with only 20 motor cars on the Island in 1901, the county council declined to act on a "grandmotherly" recommendation by Berkshire Council that every car should carry a number in a conspicuous place.

The county council did, however, warmly welcome a proposal for a Solent tunnel linking the western end of the Island with the mainland, put forward by the South Western and IW Junction Railway Company. The cost was estimated at £330,000 but the scheme failed to materialise.

King Edward VII and Sir Thomas Lipton were among those to have a narrow escape while sailing in the Solent on the new America's Cup challenger, *Shamrock II*, when she was dismasted.

Cowes Pier, erected by the district council at a cost of £10,500, was opened in March, 1902.

Sympathy was expressed with Lord Alverstone on the death of his only son, the Hon Arthur Webster, aged 28, in whose memory the Arthur Webster Hospital, Shanklin, was afterwards provided.

Newport marked the arrival of 1903 in style as the main streets were lit by electricity for the first time on New Year's Day. It was an enlightened year in more ways than one because it saw an important advance in educational administration, with a new Act resulting in the creation of education committees for the county and Newport and Ryde boroughs. Public secondary education was instituted, the Free Library Movement was firmly established and improved facilities for elementary education were provided.

Erected by the town trustees at a cost of £1,100, Brading's new town hall was opened, replacing what was reputed to be the oldest town hall in England.

Two of four escaping Parkhurst prisoners were slightly injured by rifle shots fired by warders, before all four were recaptured close to the prison.

Snowstorms, biting winds and severe frosts caused havoc with gardens and orchards at Easter in mid-April. Worse was to come as a severe gale caused considerable damage on land and sea, with the loss of four men in boating accidents off Ryde and Bembridge in September.

A Board of Trade inquiry at Newport into an application by the county council led to orders prohibiting the removal of materials from Freshwater Bay and Sandown Bay, to lessen the danger of sea erosion.

The introduction of the first motor buses on the Island came in 1904 but as the *County Press Golden Jubilee Supplement* noted: "However, neither roads nor vehicles proved suitable to ensure the establishment of permanent bus services until after the Great War."

January 13, 1904 brought bad luck to Godshill where the church was struck by lightning, causing £1,000 worth of damage — a repeat of a similar incident in January, 1778.

Lord Alverstone performed the opening ceremony of the County Technical Institute and Seely Free Library at Newport, built at a cost of £10,000, half of the money being a gift from Sir Charles Seely. Capt Seely, Sir Charles's youngest son, who had resigned his Parliamentary seat this year, mainly in opposition to the Government's fiscal policy, was re-elected as the Island's Independent MP in April.

The new Totland lifeboat rescued the captain and crew of the trading schooner *Saint*, which was stranded on Warden Ledge. And, notably, by the year's end the most powerful flashlight in the country, of 15,000 candle-power was installed at St Catherine's Lighthouse – the flash being visible on the French coast.

What was unfortunately the start of things to come was reported in 1905 – the first conviction of a motorist for being drunk in charge of a car. The driver was fined £1 with costs by Ryde Borough Magistrates and his licence suspended.

There was an early general election in 1906, when Mr Godfrey Baring won for the Liberals with a 1,561 majority over Col Hickman Morgan (Conservative). Capt Seely had by this time joined the Liberals himself and was returned as Liberal MP for Liverpool, later representing Ilkeston from 1910 until 1922.

When Rookley School won the banner for highest attendance for mixed schools in the county area it was reported that for several days one boy had carried another lad with a sprained ankle to school on his back, in order to maintain a perfect attendance record.

Captain Jack Seely (seated)

The shocks of an earthquake in Wales on June 27, 1906, were felt in the Island and recorded at Shide by Prof Milne, the eminent seismologist.

Tragedy blighted New Year's night, 1907. Ryde lifeboat was sailing home from a mission when she capsized in a heavy squall. Two of her crew, second coxswain Harry Heward and Frank Haynes, a local coastguard who had volunteered to fill a vacancy, were eventually swept away as they and seven colleagues desperately clung to lifelines from the drifting upturned boat. Incredibly the cries of the survivors were heard by a policeman at Southsea in the early hours and they were rescued, exhausted, by mainland coastguards and police.

One of the most serious fires in the history of Cowes occurred on February 18 when extensive waterside premises off Medina Road, belonging to Messrs A E Marvin and S Lallow, were destroyed, with damage estimated at £16,000.

Quarr Abbey House was purchased by the Benedictine Order of St Pierre of Solesmes, the community of monks from France who had for some time occupied Appuldurcombe House, Wroxall, and a new abbey was erected.

Two maritime disasters off the Island made the spring of 1908 unforgettable for the wrong reasons. The destroyer *Tiger* was sunk in a collision during manoeuvres off St Catherine's Point, with the loss of 36 lives. Three weeks later, on April 25, the cruiser *Gladiator* was wrecked in the Solent, near Yarmouth, after colliding during a blinding blizzard with the American liner *St Paul*. Twenty-seven of *Gladiator's* crew died.

School league tables of a kind were not unknown, since the Island received honourable mention by the Board of Education as the county with the highest percentage of average attendance of elementary schoolchildren for the country in the previous year.

Olympic Games yachting took place off Ryde, featuring entries from Norway, Sweden, Belgium, France and Britain.

Bembridge had the alarming experience of a bombardment on November 2, 1908, when live shells from 12-pounder guns fired by destroyers went far beyond their target and hurtled over houses in the sparsely populated eastern part of the district. Luckily no-one was hurt and there was no damage.

More than 1,300 Islanders received old age pensions when they were first paid on January 1, 1909.

The burial of Algernon Charles Swinburne, the great Victorian poet, who had many links with the Island, took place in April in Bonchurch churchyard close to the grave of his parents, whose home for many years was nearby East Dene.

A scheme for a funicular railway between the Esplanade, at Ventnor, and the top of St Boniface Down, was approved at a town meeting but had to be abandoned because of financial and other difficulties. Shanklin's pier pavilion, costing £4,000, was opened in the summer of 1909.

The cruiser *Gladiator* sunk in the Solent near Yarmouth

1910 – 1920

The decade that was to be ravaged by the First World War opened on an historic aerial note as the first aircraft to land on the Island touched down on Tennyson Down, Freshwater . . . by accident. "It suddenly appeared out of thunderstorm clouds over the Needles on the afternoon of July 16. Its pilot, the famous actor-aviator, Mr R Loraine, lost his way in the storm while flying over the Channel from the Bournemouth aviation meeting."

In January, 1910, there was the first of two general elections in the same year on the constitutional conflict over the veto powers of the House of Lords. Mr Douglas B Hall (Conservative) won the seat from Sir Godfrey Baring (Liberal) by a majority of 291 votes and retained it the following December with a majority of 233, this time against a new Liberal candidate, Mr Constantine Scaramanga-Ralli, whom we first encountered earlier in this book.

The Royal IW Agricultural Society declared war on wood pigeons by organising a general shoot of these "destructive birds," which became an annual event.

Cowes shipbuilders J S White and Co won a record order to build six destroyers for the Chilean Government.

Another of those maritime accidents so prevalent before the days of radar occurred in Cowes Roads in September, 1911, when the White Star liner *Olympic* was rammed by the cruiser *Hawke*, incredibly without loss of life.

The following year Mr Tommy Sopwith began experimental flights at Cowes with a water-plane launched from the yard of Saunders and Co – predecessors of Saunders-Roe.

January, 1913, saw the opening of the new territorial drill hall at Cowes, one of a series built on the Island around that time and a sign of things to come.

Islanders' reputation for patriotism was shown in all its valour during World War I with its contribution to the armed forces estimated at about 10,000 men, equivalent to almost ten percent of the population.

IW Rifles in camp at Yaverland in July, 1909

Tragically, nearly 2,000 lost their lives. More than 500 of these were from the ranks of Princess Beatrice's IW Rifles, who won renown on the battlefields of Gallipoli and Palestine, while the 5th Hants Howitzer Battery, also drawn from the Island, which fought with equal distinction in Mesopotamia, lost 75 men, nearly two-thirds of its strength.

As an article from the *County Press Golden Jubilee Supplement* so poignantly said: "The homes of all classes were bereft of brave ones, in several cases as many as three sons made the supreme sacrifice and many husbands and only sons perished."

On the home front, in 1915 the Germans reported that the Isle of Wight had been captured. Although false propaganda, this nonetheless heightened invasion fears. Trenches and other defences were hurriedly put in place and the disused Military Road extensively repaired. Wartime precautions included keeping public lighting to a minimum, the need for which was underlined one night in September, 1916, when a Zeppelin, a German airship, was seen over Ryde adjusting its course for a raid on Portsmouth.

The Island resembled an armed camp with thousands of troops from the mainland stationed here to complete their training for active service. Local hospitals also went on to a war footing and the Red Cross set up a number of their own in which nearly 10,000 sick and wounded soldiers were nursed during the war.

Following their crippling losses at Suvla Bay in the 1915 Gallipoli campaign, the IW Rifles suffered heavily again in 1917 in a major but unsuccessful offensive against the Turks in Gaza, Palestine. But with General Allenby now in command of British forces, the autumn saw fortunes reversed. The Turks were forced to retreat and the gallant Rifles played a part in the outflanking movement that resulted in a large enemy force being broken and encircled west of the Jordan in September, 1918.

Before embarking for Egypt in the November the Island soldiers who had survived four years of war then suffered from the epidemic of influenza that swept much of the world.

Islanders fully shared in the achievements of the Royal Navy and the fledgling Air Force. Admiral Viscount Jellicoe, of Ryde, was commander-in-chief of the Grand Fleet; Admiral Beatty, his successor, who received the surrender of the German Fleet, had Island associations, while Admiral Sir Gough-Calthorpe, of Ryde, received the surrender of Turkey.

Col Viscount Gort, of East Cowes, was the first peer to win this country's highest award for bravery, the Victoria Cross. A VC was also won by Capt A F B Carpenter, of Cowes, when commanding the famous blockship *HMS Vindictive* in a raid on a German submarine base on the Belgian coast. Another of these coveted medals went to an unnamed Parkhurst prisoner, who died of his wounds – one among many prisoners released to fight for their country.

For two years before the outbreak of hostilities Capt Jack Seely's burgeoning political career had seen him as Secretary for War. On his return to active service he joined the staff of Sir John French, subsequently showed inspiring leadership in command of a Canadian cavalry brigade and in 1918 was promoted to major-general. He was the author of a number of successful books, one of which, *My Horse Warrior*, was about his war experiences and his celebrated charger.

Islanders first learned of the signing of the Peace Treaty of Versailles on June 28, 1919, from a telegram received by the *County Press* 45 minutes after the event. War memorials were later erected all over the Island in tribute to those who had given their lives for their country in the bloodiest conflict the world had seen.

With the return to peace the county show resumed after being suspended during the war years, attracting an attendance of 6,000, while the first recorded instance of a honeymoon tour by aeroplane made the Cowes marriage of Miss Norah Gibson and Major E L Williams extra newsworthy.

Mr Sam Saunders, of Cowes, designed and built the country's first flying-boat; about 400 well-cared-for infants provided a novel sight at the first baby day fete organised at Newport by Island Infant Welfare Centres; and Ryde Golf Club was formed with a nine-hole course in Ryde House Park.

The year ended on a sombre note for agriculture as a serious outbreak of foot and mouth disease spread to 27 farms in Northwood, Brading and Shorwell. About 1,000 cattle were slaughtered.

1920 – 1930

Acute shortages of affordable rented housing as a result of the wartime suspension of building compelled local authorities to undertake construction of the Island's first council houses, with the assistance of a Government subsidy. Newport Corporation led the way when it accepted tenders for 28 houses on the Trafalgar Estate, costing £26,500.

The county council vetoed a proposal by one of its members to pay councillors for their travelling expenses and loss of wages. The council did act positively, though, in deciding to provide residential treatment for TB sufferers, which ultimately led to the purchase of Longford House, Havenstreet, for use as a sanatorium.

July, 1920, was the wettest and coldest July for 30 years, with 6.6 inches of rain – about three times the normal rainfall – and in complete contrast to the following year when only 5.39 inches fell in the six months to September 30.

A deputation from the Island saw the Minister of Transport on the need to improve communications with the mainland, but was told that the estimated cost of £2 million for a Solent tunnel was impracticable and that the Government was in any case against subsidies.

There was more gloom in the autumn when the Ministry ordered the temporary suspension of the Cowes-Southampton and Yarmouth-Lymington ferry services owing to a national coal strike.

But a new era in road transport started in 1921 when Vectis Buses, owned by Messrs Campbell and Dodson, started running beween Cowes and Newport, gradually extending to other routes as a forerunner to the Island-wide network of the Southern Vectis Omnibus Company.

Within a few months of the first local women magistrates being appointed, the trendsetting Ningwood and Shalfleet Women's Institute provided the first institute hall on the Island at Ningwood Hill.

Those who think twinning is a modern concept will be surprised to learn that in 1921 Princess Beatrice, the Royal Governor, and Major-General Jack Seely visited Monchy-le-

Above The Royal Yacht
Britannia on her final
departure from Cowes Week
in 1996 captured by the
lens of CP chief
photographer Chris
Thwaites

Left In September 1997 the
tide was just right for a
game of cricket on the
Brambles Bank in the
middle of the Solent

Left Wroxall residents stage
a demo in support of their
campaign for a Zebra
Crossing in the village

Left **Anthony Minghella with his Oscar at the top of Union Street, Ryde**

Far left **Annie Crutcher who won first prize in the Medina In Bloom competition with her display in Newport**

Below **Zoe Janes with her floral tribute to Princess Diana at Newport War Memorial. She had met the Princess in Great Ormond Street Hospital**

Preux, a war-devastated French village adopted by the Island, to check on the spot how best the Island could help in reconstruction. It resulted in a donation of £2,000 and many gifts in kind. Shortly after returning home the Princess showed her interest in the welfare of Island ex-servicemen when she opened the British Legion Victory Hall at Newport.

A split in the ranks of Island Conservatives and the first appearance of a Labour candidate locally were features of the General Election in November, 1922, when Sir Edgar Chatfeild-Clarke won the seat back for the Liberals.

Parkhurst prisoner Edward Conmy, 33, serving a ten-year sentence, caused a sensation when he tunnelled his way out of the jail. He was at liberty for 12 days before being recaptured at Ryde, having committed a series of audacious burglaries.

The first motor lifeboat for Island service, built at Cowes, was launched at Bembridge, where lifeboatmen had saved 182 lives during the previous 55 years of the station.

The topsy-turvey political situation saw another General Election in December, 1923. Sir Edgar Chatfeild-Clarke having resigned on health grounds, the Liberal banner was picked up by Major-General Seely, who, having first held the seat as a Conservative and then as an Independent, was successful again under new colours. It was a close run thing, though, with the Tory's Capt Peter Macdonald losing by only 90 votes. In October, 1924, Capt Macdonald defeated Major-General Seely by a record majority of 5,402 to set in train his 34-year hold on the Island constituency, during which he won a total of eight elections before retiring in 1958, aged 63.

Returning to 1923, the first Schneider Trophy air race over the Solent was won by an American pilot at an average speed of 177.38mph; the take-over of Island railways by the Southern Railway brought reduced fares and improved communications with London; Newport formed the first Rotary club on the Island and the county council budgeted for the first annual expenditure of more than £100,000.

Shortly after celebrating its 40th anniversary in November, 1924, the *County Press* began to regularly include photographs in the paper.

In his capacity as secretary of the IW Automobile Club, the paper's assistant manager, Wilfrid Brannon, wrote a letter to the editor in which he said the state of Island roads could be put into four categories – getting bad, bad, very bad and terrible.

Capt Macdonald, MP, presented a 15,000-strong petition to the Government in 1925, organised by Island Women's Institutes, protesting against the cruelty caused and injury done by the pollution of coastal waters by crude oil discharged from vessels. The Southern Railway began work on a car ferry terminal at Fishbourne and a new floating bridge was put into service at Cowes, costing £8,250.

Captain Sir Peter Macdonald

The General Strike cast its shadow over the Island in 1926 and this, coupled with the protracted miners' strike, caused considerable disruption. With no trains running, buses provided the main means of public transport and essential supplies were maintained by road transport.

Despite representations by women's organisations, the county council decided that the appointment of women police officers was "neither necessary nor desirable".

Norman Derham, son of Capt T M Derham, of East Cowes, earned the Island favourable publicity by winning a £1,000 prize for swimming the English Channel in 13 hours.

The new diocese of Portsmouth was inaugurated in 1927 and that year also saw the downland between Freshwater Bay and The Needles presented to the nation by Hallam, Lord Tennyson, for use of the public in memory of his illustrious father, whose favourite walk it was. On the other side of the Island, Professor and Mrs Poulton made a similar gift of St Helens Common in memory of their children.

At Cowes, unemployment was relieved by an order placed with J S White's by the Argentine Government for three destroyers.

With a noise that could be heard up to four miles away and in a dense cloud of dust, a massive section of cliff collapsed at Windy Corner, on July 26, 1928, leaving the famous Undercliff marine drive between Blackgang and Niton permanently blocked. In one of the largest landslides on the Island for centuries, an estimated 250,000 tons of the upper cliff went down in full view of photographers and a group of spectators.

These included a *County Press* correspondent, who was on the cliff-top about 15 yards to the west of the expected slide and wrote that he heard sharp reports like a gun. "Then, with a never-to-be-forgotten sound like thunder and the roaring of the sea, the whole mass opened and disappeared below in clouds of dust." A new road link had to be constructed over St Catherine's Down further inland to replace the 150-yard section buried to a depth of up to 20 feet.

The cattle market in St James's Square, Newport

The centuries-old custom of holding cattle markets in St James's Square, Newport, came to an end in 1928. Replacement by an enclosed market in South Street cost Newport Corporation £8,000. The IW Electric Light and Power Co launched a £200,000 scheme to supply electricity to towns and villages from a central power station at East Cowes.

The final year of this decade showed how flight had captured the public imagination. Shanklin's aerodrome at Apse – part of which still survives from its later use as a barn – was opened as the pioneer Island aviation centre, from which services to the mainland were developed.

Sir Alan Cobham's first air display at Somerton, Cowes, was followed in September, 1929, by another epic race for the Schneider Trophy. Some 70,000 spectators crowded the north coast of the Island and watched the British team beat Italy's greatest fliers. Flying Officer H R D Waghorn was the individual winner at an average speed in his streamlined seaplane of 326.63mph.

Sandown Canoe Lake and Ventnor Winter Gardens, the latter secured by the purchase of the old vicarage site, were among new attractions for visitors. At Cowes, the district council accepted with gratitude Capt Ward's magnificent gift to the town of Northwood House as a municipal centre and public park.

1930 – 1940

The loss of Sir Harry Seagrave after breaking the world water speed record on Lake Windermere in June, 1930, was specially mourned at East Cowes where his boat, *Miss England II*, was built by Saunders-Roe Ltd to the design of Mr F Cooper, of Newport.

The same month, Sir A V Roe, a leading figure in aviation, who had gone into partnership with Samuel Saunders to form the restructured company, predicted at the Island's first air pageant, at Shanklin Aerodrome, that aircraft would play an important part in the development of the Island.

Newport Corporation created a precedent by electing Mrs E R Chandler the Island's first woman mayor.

The census in April, 1931, recorded a local population of 88,454. This was 6,212 less than the figure ten years before, but that had been taken in June when visitors were included.

County bowlers reached the final of the Middleton Cup, the county championship, in 1931, before losing to the holders, Surrey, by 129 shots to 108 but there was a major consolation when E P Topp, of Ryde, won the national singles title.

Industrial strife broke out on the buses as 100 conductors and a few drivers of Southern Vectis struck in a dispute over the sacking of two colleagues. Within a week services were virtually back to normal with new employees taking the place of the strikers.

The Island made its contribution to the sweeping win of the National Government in October, 1931, by returning Capt Macdonald with a majority of 23,089 in the first straight local fight with a Socialist candidate – Capt J E Drummond.

Camp Hill Prison was converted to a Borstal Institution for young offenders after apparently failing to come up to official expectations as an experimental prison for hardened criminals. Within a few months two of the inmates escaped and crossed to the mainland – something that no escaping prisoner had managed to do before from an Island establishment.

A new era of local government came into being in 1933 with the number of district councils on the Island being reduced from nine to six, as Shanklin and Sandown amalgamated, Cowes and East Cowes did likewise and St Helens came under the Borough of Ryde, all "in the interests of economical and efficient administration." As part of the streamlining nearly half of the rural district was absorbed within the new town boundaries.

Although it was its 50th anniversary there were no golden celebrations for the Royal IW Agricultural Society. No show was held due to the visit of the Royal Show to Southampton and acute depression in the farming industry.

August saw the opening of Ryde's splendid Western Garden extension, made possible by the purchase and demolition by the Corporation of the Royal Pier Hotel and adjacent buildings. Ryde continued to grab the headlines with the opening of an aerodrome on the outskirts of the town next to where the Tesco store is today. The start of regular air services from there and Somerton to Portsmouth and London marked an important advance for the Island.

Signs of returning prosperity in 1933 were marked by a fall in unemployment, improving conditions for farming and manufacturing and a record influx of visitors. Two ceremonies attracted international interest. One was the opening to the public of Nansen Hill, between Shanklin and Ventnor, as a memorial provided by Mr J Howard Whitehouse to the famous Arctic explorer after whom it was named. The second was the unveiling on Cowes Parade of a bronze plaque commemorating the sailing from the port 300 years before of the *Ark* and *Dove* with the first British settlers for Maryland, USA.

Major-General the Rt Hon Jack Seely was created a baron in the King's birthday honours with the title of Lord Mottistone. This was in recognition of his distinguished service to the country and Empire as soldier; Parliamentarian and public servant. He held the position of Lord Lieutenant of Hampshire from 1918 until his death in 1947.

Lord Mottistone was also an outstanding figure as a leader of the National Savings movement. Another indication of his national stature was his appointment as chairman of the famous Wembley Stadium, opened in 1923. As a man of action he was devoted to the lifeboat service. He joined the Brook lifeboat as a young man and was appointed coxswain in 1933. He also held the presidency of the IW Lifeboat Board.

The summer season of 1934 was another record-breaker in terms of visitors and sunshine. Sandown-Shanklin Urban District Council did its part for tourist entertainment by opening Sandown's new pier pavilion and Shanklin's enlarged town hall.

Membership of the county council was increased for the first time from the original 40 to 48 and included the first woman county councillor in Mrs M C Barton, of East Cowes – no relation to another Barton, Morris, who was to become leader of the authority many years later.

Southern Vectis opened its new central depot and garage at Nelson Road, Newport, and progress continued in the air as a daily service began in May between the Island and the Midlands. The following August the first air mail service was launched linking Somerton and

Above Joanna Adams and daughter Emily, of Brighstone, with their dog Bonnie who has a special frame to enable her to stay mobile

Far left The Rev Andrew Froud at St Edmund's Church, Wootton, with newly married Tim and Mandy Herley. He dropped off from a sponsored cycle ride to perform the ceremony

Left The Boxing Day Hunt meeting at Carisbrooke Castle

Above A snow plough gritting its own way out of trouble on Brading Down in December, 1997

Right Prince Charles talks to East Cowes Grange School teacher Susie Rawlings during his unscheduled walkabout on his way to Osborne House in July, 1999

the Midlands. Road users had something to celebrate as the county council freed the Yar Bridge at Yarmouth from tolls about a year after purchasing it.

In 1935 there was a sinister hint of things to come when members of the Seaview unit of the British Union of Fascists held a meeting at St Helens and were told that their national leader, Sir Oswald Mosley, "commanded the love and esteem of 100,000 people."

One of the Island's pioneers of cinema, Mr Albert Salter, was a leading member of a syndicate which carried out the redevelopment that year of the Medina Cinema in Newport High Street. He had begun showing moving pictures in 1897 at the Medina Hall, on the site of which the new 1,000-seater super cinema was built – later occupied by the Picturedrome.

In 1937 a detachment from the IW Rifles attended the coronation in London of King George VI and Queen Elizabeth. This was the year in which the Rifles' distinguished and gallant role as an infantry unit came to a close. It was converted to a heavy artillery unit with the important task of manning some of the Island's batteries as part of the outer defences of Portsmouth and Southampton.

The new 530 Coast Regiment, RA, Princess Beatrice's IW Rifles, was called out for eight or nine days during 1938 at the time of the Munich crisis and the first lectures on air raid defence were held at Osborne House by a specially trained instructress from the British Red Cross Society.

On August 25, 1939, the Rifles were ordered to report to their gunsites and this time there was to

The new Medina Cinema in Newport High Street

be no reprieve from hostilities. As the *County Press* said: "Like the rest of the country the Island received the announcement on September 3 that a State of War existed between England and Germany with a certain sense of relief – having realised it was a necessity in order that Hitlerism and all its pagan policies should be banished from the earth."

1940 – 1950

The author's childhood memories of the early years of the war include the seven towering pylons or masts, ranging from 250ft to 350ft, on St Boniface Down at Ventnor. Few Islanders had heard of radar in those days but this massive installation for the RAF was part of a network of radar stations along the South Coast to give advance warning of German planes approaching across the Channel.

The radar masts on St Boniface Down, near Ventnor

Another vivid memory is of the hot, sunny day when, from my grandparents' garden at Wroxall, I watched as the Luftwaffe attacked the St Boniface station. I could not recall the date but I was confident I would find the answer in *Battle in the Skies Over the Isle of Wight* by H J T Leal. It was August 12, 1940. Twenty Ju88 bombers took part in the attack and the radar station was put out of action for several days, but, as Mr Leal's book repeatedly shows, Ventnor radar continued to play a vital role in the battle of the skies.

Recently I read an eye-witness account of a WAAF who was operating the telephone exchange at the radar station during the attack. She courageously stayed at her post until a sergeant shouted to her to go to the air raid shelter, which she reached after jumping over an unexploded bomb. Down in the shelter she found a high-ranking officer who was visiting the station. He asked her why she was not wearing a tin hat – and she told him there were not enough to go round.

Among the pictures in Mr Leal's book is one of members of the Royal Observer Corps' Mount Joy post at Newport. In the line-up I recognised four *County Press* employees: Mr Sibbick, the editor, who was chief observer at the post; Reg Allen, a printer and brother of Gerald Allen who was to succeed their father, Henry, as chief reporter; Percy Appel, the jobbing room foreman, and that indestructible veteran of the Boer and First World wars, Bob Lawn, senior.

Beaches along the Island's coast, accustomed to welcoming visitors, became no-go areas with barbed wire along cliff-tops and criss-cross ironwork defences at low water to help repel an invasion.

In September, 1940, Mrs Dorothy O'Grady, a Sandown landlady – and former Soho prostitute – was arrested at Yaverland for constantly snooping around prohibited coastal areas. She was later convicted of treason and sentenced to hang, but escaped with a 14-year jail sentence after a successful appeal.

Mrs O'Grady, the only British woman sentenced to death for spying during the war, was released in 1950 and returned to Sandown after serving nine years of her sentence. She died in 1985, aged 87, while a resident of Porter Court, Lake, still protesting her innocence and claiming that her downfall was due to her being an exhibitionist living out a fantasy by pretending that she was a spy.

This version was challenged by former Island MP Barry Field who said that evidence at her trial, released under the 30-year rule, showed that on arrest a swastika badge was found on the inside of Mrs O'Grady's coat and that she was carrying maps of the Island with its main military installations marked.

Captured German documents showed that at one stage the Island was earmarked as a possible springboard from which to launch an invasion of the mainland. Little wonder, then, in a repeat of what happened in the First World War, that the Island quickly resembled an armed camp with thousands of troops stationed here, first as a precautionary measure against an invasion and then to continue training before being posted abroad. A ride in an army truck was a coveted treat for a youngster in those days. Many Island families provided billets for soldiers and wartime homes for evacuee children from mainland cities like Portsmouth.

Rationing was an inevitable consequence of the war and in January, 1940, the *County Press* reported the introduction of rationing of bacon, ham, butter and sugar. The weekly amounts allowed per person were four ounces of uncooked bacon or ham, three-and-a-half ounces if cooked (free of bone); a quarter-of-a-pound of butter; and three-quarters-of-a-pound of sugar.

Meat, clothing, sweets and petrol were among other things affected as ration books and coupons became a way of life.

The Island's wartime grapevine spread the news like wildfire when the cross-Solent passenger ferry *Portsdown* was ripped in two by a mine as she sailed from Portsmouth to Ryde on September 19, 1941. The disaster happened in the Swashway just outside Portsmouth Harbour and claimed more than 20 lives, most of them servicemen and women. A similar number survived the sinking.

Whether the *Portsdown* hit a mine laid by a German plane or one of our own that had drifted into the shipping lane is still an open question, as an exhaustively researched account of the incident by author Ken Phillips, of Apse Heath, shows in his book *Shipwreck! Broken on the Wight*.

Censorship prevented the *County Press* from reporting the disaster at the time. But there were a succession of death notices in the paper and readers must have put two and two together from these, particularly one saying "Died whilst travelling to Ryde . . ."

Island coastal towns became a target for vicious so-called hit and run raids by German fighters and bombers, but Cowes and East Cowes, with the J S White shipyard on either side of the River Medina and the Saunders-Roe aircraft factory, were the targets of the most sustained attack on the night of May 4-5, 1942.

In two raids the Luftwaffe dropped about 200 tons of bombs, inflicting heavy damage and killing 70 people in the twin towns and a further ten at Newport. The destruction and loss of life would have been even greater but for the heroic defence by anti-aircraft gunners aboard the Polish warship *Blyskawica*. Their sustained barrage and the smokescreen laid from the ship caused many raiders to drop their bombs off target or into the sea. She was berthed at White's for a refit, having had a narrow escape a week earlier when bombs fell so close to her that the gangplank to the jetty was blown into the air and fell across the ship.

Cowes and East Cowes have never forgotten the debt of gratitude owed to the *Blyskawica* and her crew, some of whom married local girls and settled on the Island after the war. Ceremonies are still held to commemorate the anniversary of the night the ship put up such a courageous fight and the organisation Friends of the Blyskawica was formed in 1997 to help finance the restoration of the vessel, which became a floating museum in her homeland.

Was the *County Press* the target for a German bomb in 1943? That intriguing possibility was raised by Mrs Freda Snowdon, of Ash Tree Way, Nettlestone, when she told of the miraculous escape her mother had during a raid. Enemy planes swooped on Newport at about 7.30am early in April. Mrs Snowdon's mother, Freda Salter, was in bed in the flat above the electricity company's offices next door to the *County Press* when the property was blown up. She was cut to ribbons from head to toe but incredibly no bones were broken.

"She went down between the bed and wall and her one thought was to hang on to the bag containing money she had collected the day before to bank for a great-aunt at Ningwood who had sold some cows," said Mrs Snowdon. "Because she realised she was sinking in the rubble she used a piece of lath to make a hole so she could breathe."

Mrs Snowdon, who was working for the Air Ministry in the north when the raid happened, said she was told that because the devastation was so great a rescue team who went by said "Poor Mrs Salter". They had assumed that no-one could possibly have survived. Fortunately for her mother, a lad who worked in the electricity offices with her, rushed across from the toilets under the Guildhall

The bomb damaged shops next to the *County Press* in Newport High Street

opposite and with the help of a soldier managed to pull her from what others had thought was her tomb.

Mrs Snowdon said her father, who was working as a cinema manager in Southsea at the time, told her that there was strong speculation that the bomb was intended for the *County Press* works as part of an attack on selected targets in Newport, like creameries and food stores and Morey's timber yard which produced components for Mosquito fighter-bombers.

"But the bomb intended for the *County Press* went through the Medina Cinema and exploded in the shops next door." The paper's report of the incident was restricted by censorship which prevented it, for example, from even naming Newport. Instead a headline referred to: Damage and Casualties in Market Town. There could have been few, if any, readers who were not aware, however, that the report referred to the Island's capital. Fifteen people were killed in the raid, including three workers at the timber yard.

Despite the loss of life, there were some lucky escapes, including that of Mrs Ena Blee, wife of the *County Press* caretaker. She was in bed in a top floor room and jumped out on hearing cannon fire. Moments later a one-hundredweight steel showcard printing machine, hurled into the air from a drapery shop next door to the electricity company premises, crashed through the roof on to Mrs Blee's bed with such force that it knocked a hole in the floorboards.

Island farming was on an emergency footing under the War Agricultural Executive Committee (WAEC). A shortage of labour was one of the main problems, although members of the Women's Land Army splendidly helped to fill the breach as farmers here played their part to make Britain self-sufficient in food. Convicts, Italian prisoners-of-war and later German POW also worked on Island farms.

"Dig for Victory" was the slogan to encourage everyone with a garden or allotment to grow the maximum amount of vegetables and fruit. Advertisements in the *County Press* urged Islanders to eat more potatoes, to reduce to a minimum the need to import wheat from the other side of the Atlantic on merchant ships at perpetual risk from German submarines. (It was well over a decade before rationing completely disappeared and in 1947 the *County Press* was involved in a scheme that saw kind-hearted Australians sending food parcels to needy elderly Islanders).

Because of its seaside location the Island made an ideal training ground for rehearsing beach assaults. Shanklin Chine became a familiar haunt for Royal Marine commandos, for example, and the Chine played a leading part in another enterprise which signalled that the war was not going Adolf Hitler's way. This was PLUTO – Pipe-Line Under The Ocean – a complex and dauntingly difficult scheme to supply Allied forces with fuel after they had gained a foothold in France in the summer of 1944.

The final section on this side of the Channel of the pipeline to Cherbourg was routed through the Chine and part of it still remains. The project also involved laying a pipeline from Dungeness in Kent to Boulogne. Island author Adrian Searle has written the definitive book on PLUTO, an operation so secret that troops assigned to carry out some of the preparations actually thought they were going abroad when they embarked on the mainland for a voyage that turned out to be much shorter than they had expected.

In the run-up to D-Day, June 5, 1944, there were an estimated 17,000 troops training on the Island, including those from the USA, Canada and France. Many others were in protective anchorages off the Island waiting to set out for the Normandy beaches. The noise of the intensive naval bombardment and air attacks that accompanied the invasion could be heard on the Island.

The ringing of bells, the crack of fireworks, the glow of bonfires, the flashing of searchlights, no longer concentrating on enemy raiders, all added to the memorable celebration of VE Day – Victory in Europe Day – on May 8, 1945.

Many Island servicemen and women paid the supreme sacrifice and never returned to their native shores. The war had also taken its toll on the Island itself with 125 air raids in which 1,748 high explosive bombs and landmines fell, in addition to thousands of incendiaries and oil bombs. More than 200 men, women and children were killed.

The war against Japan continued, until the dropping of the atom bombs on Nagasaki and Hiroshima in August, 1945, brought hostilities to an abrupt end, not to say an horrendous one as the full implications of nuclear war dawned. Many Islanders had fought against the fanatical Japanese foe and the comradeship they then established lives on in the Burma Star Association, whose founding patron was the Island's late Governor, Earl Mountbatten, the wartime Supreme Allied Commander for South East Asia.

Among those not to return from war in the Far East were two army officers with strong Island links who both won Britain's highest honour for military valour, the Victoria Cross. Lt Claud Raymond, born at Mottistone, and Lt George Cairns, members of whose family live at Brighstone, were both members of the legendary Chindits. They showed outstanding bravery despite appalling injuries in securing key positions against ferocious Japanese opposition.

In 1947 there were signs of reconciliation at least as far as Germany was concerned, when about 550 German POW out of approximately 700 held on the Island were entertained by a concert party at the Medina Cinema, Newport. Entertainment was the last thing on the mind of an escaped Parkhurst prisoner, who, after stealing a dinghy and oars, was spotted by a Fleet Air Arm pilot desperately clinging to a cable buoy half-a-mile off Egypt Point at Cowes. He was rescued by the Royal Navy.

Weatherwise, 1947 was notable for the severest winter since the great snowfall of 1881 and a summer heatwave that led to serious milk and water shortages as the Island's holiday trade returned to pre-war proportions.

The following year saw the opening of Cowes Secondary School, built at a cost of £65,000, while the New Year of 1949 came in like a lion, with severe gales causing havoc to powerlines. Farm roofs at Ryde were torn off by a mini-tornado.

Two Yarmouth brothers, Stanley and Colin Smith, caught the imagination of the whole country that summer when they completed a 43-day crossing of the Atlantic in a 20ft yacht, the *Nova Espero*, which they had built themselves. The sons of the then Yarmouth lifeboat coxwain, Stanley Smith, they relied on an ex-RAF compass as their only technical aid and their nearest thing to a wet suit was a trenchcoat. Two years later Stanley Jnr, sailed the *Nova Espero* to New York with a friend, Charles Violet.

1950 – 1960

"Polio Isle." It was sensational headlines like this in some national papers in the summer of 1950 that brought the Island's growing post-war holiday trade revival to a calamitous stop. Many hoteliers, guest house owners and holiday camp proprietors lost hundreds of bookings as intended visitors stayed away, frightened by stories splashed by Fleet Street that the Isle of Wight was in the grip of a potentially deadly epidemic of poliomyelitis, or infantile paralysis as it was also known because of its prevalence among young people.

The panic reached its peak in the August when the Island's MP, Sir Peter Macdonald, issued a statement criticising the sensational treatment being given to the local situation and pointing out that other resorts on the mainland were also experiencing cases of polio.

But reports in the *County Press* showed how seriously the authorities were treating the outbreak, with the Fairlee Infectious Diseases Hospital, Newport, appealing for extra nurses to help an over-stretched staff. One ward at the Royal IW County Hospital, Ryde, and two at St Mary's Hospital, Newport, were made available for cases past the acute and highly infectious stage.

Swimming pools were closed, extra iron lungs used to help sufferers with breathing difficulties were flown to the Island and the re-opening of schools after the summer holiday was delayed. A subsequent report by Dr W S Wallace, medical officer of health for the IW, showed that during the outbreak there had been 54 paralytic and 41 non-paralytic cases of polio, with three people dying from the disease.

"Although the total number of cases did not justify the term epidemic the notice which was taken of the disease by the Press made one feel that a pestilence had visited the Island," said Dr Wallace. "The fact that we were the first holiday resort to have sufficient cases to justify mention in the Press, together with bad initial handling of publicity, was responsible for a Press campaign which, from the economic point of view, was ruinous to the IW season." His deputy, Dr John Mills, actually contracted polio as he too worked tirelessly to combat the spread of the virus.

This decade was one of triumph and turmoil for Saunders-Roe, the aircraft manufacturers, whose long-established headquarters are at East Cowes. No one who saw the maiden flight of the Princess flying boat in August, 1952, will forget the sight of this majestic 140-ton leviathan of the sky but, having been six years in the making, she and her two sister Princesses were destined for a sad end.

They were cocooned while development problems with the engines were overcome, but this did not happen in time to convince potential operators of their viability. At one point there was speculation that the "Sleeping Princesses" as they became known might be used by the Americans as test beds for atomic-powered engines, but nothing came of this and they were eventually sold off for scrap.

One of the three Saunders-Roe Princess flying boats built in the early 1950s

Other revolutionary projects, such as the company's rocket-jet fighter, the SR 177, also failed to take off commercially after the then Government cancelled an order for nine aircraft in favour of guided missiles. This decision led to massive redundancies in the late 1950s, with around 1,500 employees losing their jobs.

Even so, Saunders-Roe, with its proud past in marine and aviation innovation, also has a distinguished place in modern British manufacturing history. It had a pioneering partnership with Sir Christopher Cockerell, inventor of the hovercraft, which ultimately led to huge cross-Channel car-carrying craft. The company also had a spearhead role in earning Britain a place, albeit comparatively short-lived, in the rocket age with the Black Knight guided missile, which had its first firing on the Woomera range in Australia in September, 1958.

The 1950s were a traumatic time for Island railways. The Ventnor West to Merstone line was closed in September, 1952. Newport to Freshwater and Bembridge to Brading followed suit a year later and the Sandown to Newport line via Merstone was shut in 1956. All had become unviable as car ownership grew and competition from bus services also took its toll.

Seaview suffered a literal blow in 1951 when a gale destroyed its suspension pier.

An indication of the tough disciplinary regimes still operating in prisons came in a November, 1953, report of how a board of visiting magistrates sentenced a Parkhurst prisoner to six strokes of the cat o' nine tails for attacking a prison officer. This was the last recorded occasion of the "cat" being used at Parkhurst. The last recorded case at an Island jail of a birching was at Camp Hill in 1961.

Ventnor's newly reconstructed Royal Victoria Pier was re-opened in 1955. It cost £122,000 and was described as the most modern in Britain. Sadly, this did not prevent it falling into neglect again and, despite ambitious rebuilding plans, it was demolished in 1993 having never recovered from the effects of a mystery blaze which caused an estimated £500,000 damage in September, 1985.

The Island's worst peacetime disaster occurred in November, 1957, when a large flying-boat crashed into a chalkpit at Shalcombe Farm, near the Calbourne to Freshwater road. The plane, outward bound from Southampton for Las Palmas and Madeira, via Lisbon, immediately burst into flames. Of the 50 passengers and eight crew, 43 lost their lives in the holocaust and two more of the passengers died in hospital. The tragedy, involving a Short Solent aircraft owned by Aquila Airways, was widely regarded as having hastened the end of flying boats being used for large-scale passenger services

Life was not all doom and gloom. In the same month a Newport milkman called Terry Perkins won a talent contest at the town's Medina Cinema, later the Picturedrome. His success led to a change of name and fortune as the newly-styled Craig Douglas shot to pop stardom, being voted the most outstanding new discovery in Britain in 1958. Altogether between 1959 and 1962 Craig enjoyed a dozen hit singles, selling five million records in the process. His greatest success came in the summer of 1959 when his recording of *Only Sixteen* topped the charts for six weeks. Unlike many young singers of the era, who disappeared from show business, Craig established himself as a highly professional all-round entertainer, still in demand 40 years on.

1960 – 1970

Wet, wet, wet was the only way to describe 1960 when rainfall totals in excess of 50 inches were recorded at several locations, making it the wettest year since the *County Press* first appeared in 1884. There was widespread flooding and parts of Newport resembled a lake on October 1 when a heavy thunderstorm was followed by a cloudburst. At nearby Chillerton 3.1in of rain fell between 3am and 4am. Newport's storm drains and brooks feeding into the harbour were overwhelmed, turning roads and streets into rivers.

A young mother was saved from drowning after a boat taking her to dry ground from her flooded home in Lower St James's Street capsized. A pig was spotted swimming for its life in Crocker Street. Mew Langton's brewery was flooded and barrels of beer floated into Newport Harbour. At Shanklin, which also suffered flooding, an elderly woman rang a handbell to summon help as water poured into her home.

The bottom of Hunnyhill, Newport in October, 1960

The winter of 1962-63 saw the Island gripped in the big freeze. During the 70 days from December 23, 1962, to March 2, 1963, an air frost was registered in some parts of the Island every day, with daytime maximum temperatures at Ryde only twice reaching and never topping 40 degrees fahrenheit. The lowest temperature recorded during that period was 15 degrees below freezing. Snow clearance alone cost the county council more than £44,000 and the severe and prolonged frosts took a heavy toll of road foundations and surfaces.

Reporter Leslie Rodaway was quickly on the scene on May 6, 1962, when a Dakota aircraft crashed in thick fog on St Boniface Down, Ventnor. His harrowing report told how eight of the 14 passengers and two of the crew of three were killed when the Channel Air Services flight to Portsmouth and Southend came to its tragic end. All survivors were seriously injured. First on the scene was Mr Edward Price, a Wroxall farmworker, who regardless of his own safety helped passengers who had been thrown clear from the burning wreckage.

Largely due to the tireless efforts of the Island MP, Ald Mark Woodnutt, there was brighter news on the industrial front in 1964 as Decca Radar, a world leader in radar and electronics, opened new factory units and laboratories on the site of the former Somerton Airport at Cowes. Decca had arrived at Somerton three years earlier, where it established a radar testing site.

By the time the splendid new facilities were opened the company was employing 600, many of whom had lost jobs as a result of redundancies at Saunders-Roe which had had such a depressing effect on Island unemployment. The Somerton site was later taken over by Plessey Radar, then Siemens and more recently by British Aerospace, having become one of the largest and most vital parts of the Island's manufacturing base.

A 96-year history of treating patients suffering from chest diseases, in particular tuberculosis, came to an end in 1964 with the closure of the renowned Royal National Hospital on the outskirts of Ventnor. After the demolition of the long and narrow building, where some 50,000 patients had been treated over the years, the hospital's magnificent cliff-top grounds became the site of Ventnor Botanic Garden – officially opened by Lord Mountbatten in 1972.

At Bembridge Airport, Britten-Norman was playing its part in the revival of the Island's employment scene through the development of the Islander air taxi, with its remarkable short take-off and landing capabilities. The Islander made its maiden flight in June 1965 – a triumph for those visionaries after whom the company was named, the late John Britten and co-founder Desmond Norman.

Despite this proving a world-beater in terms of sales, owners of the Bembridge company have never found life easy in the capital-sapping and competitive aircraft manufacturing business. There have been two periods of receivership but, thanks mainly to the Swiss-based Pilatus company, Britten-Norman has survived and since July, 1998, has reverted to its original title under another change of ownership. The resilience of the multi-purpose Islander has never been in doubt, with sales of it and the military variant, the Defender, and the three-engine Trislander, totalling more than 1,200 in well over 100 countries.

A few weeks after the Islander made its debut Hovertravel started the first regular scheduled cross-Solent hovercraft service between, Ryde and Southsea. There had been an experimental service the previous summer to and from Appley, Ryde, and Eastney, Portsmouth, and an eight-day trial by the British Hovercraft Corporation – the Westland-owned successors to Saunders-Roe – between Ryde and Southsea in August, 1962. Hovertravel has carried more than 17 million passengers across the Solent since 1965, while in 1968 Princess Margaret inaugurated car-ferry hovercraft services between Dover and France with the SRN 4.

In July, 1966, British Rail's Seaspeed company began a hovercraft passenger service between Cowes and Southampton, followed the next year by a service between Cowes and Portsmouth. A new-style sidewall hovercraft built by Hovermarine, of Southampton, was used when Seaspeed began operating between Ryde and Portsmouth in 1968.

A proud centuries-old tradition of shipbuilding at Cowes came to a sad end in November, 1965, as J S White's closed its shipyard section with the loss of nearly 400 jobs. A full-page article by Vic Jackson, the *County Press* reporter in the port, recalled that for more than 300 years vessels had been built on the site of the yard – since 1798 by White's. The company continued with engineering but was taken over by the American Carrier Company in 1972 and five years later renamed Elliott Turbomachinery, the title of the international company whose equipment it produced.

At one time Elliott's had a 850-strong workforce and won the Queen's Award to Industry for export achievement. It then became part of another American conglomerate, which shocked the Island by closing the company in November, 1981, with the loss of approximately 500 jobs. The White's name was reborn as the title of the industrial and commercial complex set up on the 12.5-acre site in a joint and successful venture by the county council and private enterprise to create new jobs.

Railway closures climaxed in 1966 with the demise of the Cowes to Newport and the Newport to Ryde St John's lines in February. The Cowes to Newport line had been the first to be opened in the Island in June, 1862. Now all that remained of the Island's steam age was running between Ryde Pier Head and Ventnor. In April, 1966, that line was truncated by the closure of the Shanklin to Ventnor section – a blow from which Ventnor has never really recovered. From January 1 to March 20 the following year the Island was without rail services as the Shanklin to Ryde Pier Head line was electrified in readiness for operating a fleet of refurbished and modified elderly London Transport Underground rolling stock.

Steam did make a comeback, however, thanks to the Wight Locomotive Society and the IW Steam Railway Co. Centred on Havenstreet, a great attraction for railway buffs, tourists and Islanders has been built up into a nationally acclaimed steam railway, which now has connections at Smallbrook Halt, Ryde, with the electrified service.

Radical proposals for Island education, in line with preparations for the national switch to the comprehensive system and the ending of selection at 11-plus, were put foward for wide-scale consultation with parents in the autumn of 1966. These foreshadowed the phasing in from September, 1971, of a three-stage system of schools – a primary section for five to nine-year-olds; new-style middle schools for nine to 13-year-olds, and what were to become high schools for those over 13. The changes, of which the county education officer designate, Mr William Barrett, was the architect, won Government approval in the summer of 1967 with a rare bouquet from Whitehall.

A third Island prison, called Albany after the name of the redundant barracks site on which it was built near Parkhurst jail, was opened in 1967. Two years later Parkhurst was in the headlines for all the wrong reasons when a riot erupted in October, 1969. Some of the most violent criminals in the country took temporary control of a recreational block, barricading themselves in and taking seven prison officers hostage. Although the disturbance lasted only about 30 minutes, some ten officers and 20 prisoners were injured in the pitched battle that took place as staff fought to win back control of the block and rescue their colleagues.

There was a unique sequel to the riot the following year when, for the first time, a sitting of Hampshire Assizes took place on the Island. Because of the security implications in taking a group of high risk prisoners to Winchester where the court normally sat, Newport's historic Guildhall was chosen. The ten-week sitting concluded with the conviction of seven prisoners, who were given additional sentences ranging from 18 months to six years for their part in the riot. Two other prisoners were cleared of all charges. Outbreaks of serious violence and rooftop demonstrations were to become a regular occurrence for some years to come at Parkhurst and Albany and to a lesser extent Camp Hill.

January, 1968, struck an embarrassing note for the Royal Navy when the submarine *HMS Alliance* grounded on Bembridge Ledge as she returned from exercises in the Western Approaches to her base at Gosport. The 1,120-ton vessel was only slightly damaged but was firmly wedged on the treacherous ledge some 400 yards from the shore opposite the Crab and Lobster Hotel, which became the base for reporters and cameramen covering the story. After being stranded for ten days the sub was winched off at high tide. More than half of the 65-strong crew had been taken off by helicopter and Bembridge lifeboat took out provisions for those left aboard.

The Island found itself thrust on to the world stage over the August Bank Holiday in 1969

when the famous American singer Bob Dylan topped the bill at a pop festival on a farm at Woodside Bay, Wootton. An estimated 100,000 fans came from abroad and all over the country, swamping Wootton and neighbouring towns. For a few days flower power reigned supreme and although the event passed off relatively trouble-free there were complaints of among other things, nude dancing, hippies lying across pavements, a Ryde cemetery being used as a toilet and two fans barging into a Wootton woman's home and having a bath despite being refused entry.

In reality this was just a taster of what was to come a year later as organisers Fiery Creations staged an even larger festival at Afton Down, on the outskirts of Freshwater.

1970 – 1980

If the death of the world's most powerful monarch, Queen Victoria, at Osborne soon after the turn of the century was the most significant single event reported by the *County Press*, then the pop festival held at East Afton Farm, Freshwater, must surely be the runner-up in terms of international impact.

For five days at the end of August, 1970, this was where it was all happening as an estimated 250,000 fans from all parts of the world converged on the acres of tranquil grassland beneath Afton Down, which was turned into a massive arena and canvas town complete with shops, bars and toilets.

Billed as the world's greatest gathering of love, music and peace, the festival stars included Jimmy Hendrix, Joan Baez, Miles Davis, Donovan and Leonard Cohen. Learning from the lessons of the Wootton festival the year before, the authorities drew up an agreement signed by promoters Fiery Creations laying down strict conditions for the event. These included the provision of 1,200 toilet closets, compared to the 80 provided at Wootton; 1,800 feet of urinals; an adequate water supply; and stringent compliance with food hygiene regulations.

For all these well-laid plans a shanty encampment called Desolation Row quickly emerged in an adjoining hedgerow, occupied by those who either could not afford or wanted no part of the official tented accommodation.

Shops in Freshwater and Totland found their shelves stripped of food and drink as they tried to keep pace with the demands of thousands of hungry hippies. Compton Bay and other nearby beaches experienced stripping of a different kind as some festival-goers bathed and sunbathed in the nude. Many Islanders swelled the festival numbers, some becoming part-time hippies and at least one Newport mother failed to recognise her flower power son when he spoke to her. Cross-Solent ferry operators had a bonanza and so too did Southern Vectis running a shuttle service from Ryde to the festival.

Extra police were drafted in from the mainland and courts were in continuous session at Newport dealing mainly with drug-related offences. One pusher was reported to have been selling curry powder as cannabis and 1,000 gallons of tea and coffee was poured away after fears it had been contaminated with LSD.

The Isle of Wight pop festival in August, 1970

Hell's Angels were relieved of an assortment of vicious looking weapons before they were allowed to board ferries at Portsmouth but it was a group of French anarchists who were to prove the main problem as they led attempts to gatecrash the arena from the overlooking hillside.

This hillside had become a free grandstand for thousands of fans and was blamed by the organisers for the festival turning into a financial flop when they were faced with hundreds of disgruntled creditors.

Fiery Creations was, in reality, brothers Ronald and Raymond Foulk (the latter, incidentally, had previously worked for the *County Press* as a compositor). Their company was compulsorily wound up in the High Court early in 1971 after a judge heard that negotiations for the sale of its rights in a film of the festival – its only asset – had come to nothing. One direct outcome of the Wootton and East Afton festivals was the 1971 Isle of Wight Act giving local authorities powers to control overnight assemblies of more than 5,000 and this was tightened up in the wake of problems caused by large Bank Holiday scooter rallies in the 1980s.

The Island grabbed national and international headlines again in October, 1970, when it had a narrow escape from an oil pollution disaster. As it was, 13 crewman lost their lives as two heavily laden Liberian-registered tankers collided six miles off St Catherine's Point. After an explosion, fire immediately engulfed the 43,000-ton *Pacific Glory* and she was badly holed. She was carrying 70,000 tons of crude oil from Africa to Rotterdam. The second vessel, the 46,000-ton *Allegro*, with a cargo of 93,000 gallons of crude oil destined for Fawley, Southampton, sustained only superficial damage.

Flames from the *Pacific Glory* leapt 80ft casting a red glow in the night sky south of the Island and black smoke billowed several hundred feet. Royal Navy and merchant ships picked up the 29 survivors despite the crippled vessel being surrounded by burning oil. At one time it was feared she would sink but tugs managed to tow her to a sandbank off Dunnose Point, near Shanklin. After more than 36 hours the courageous firefighters brought the blaze under control and Dutch and Belgian salvage tugs took over.

The 1970s witnessed some extraordinary weather. June 10, 1971, was probably the wettest day in the Island's meteorological history, with 4.79in of rain recorded at Shide, near Newport. There was heavy snow in 1978 and 1979 with drifts of up to 20ft deep and Ventnor and some villages were temporarily cut off.

The unforgettable summer of 1976 saw Island beaches resemble the South of France as, from May to September, Sandown basked in 1,374 hours of sunshine and Totland Bay 1,399 hours, with 377 hours during July alone – the sunniest calendar month to date. On the reverse side of the coin the heatwave and drought turned the Island countryside into a tinderbox, with firemen on almost continuous call-out tackling grass and heath fires.

Having gained its separate county status in the Victorian era, the Island launched a fierce campaign, backed by a 15,000-strong petition, to retain its jealously guarded independence in the face of proposals as part of a national re-organisation of local government to link it again with Hampshire. Victory came in 1972 with a Government decision to allow the Island to carry on running its own affairs.

There were changes at district council level, though, and 1974 saw a streamlining exercise in which Ryde, Newport and Cowes came under a newly-created Medina council, with Sandown-Shanklin, Ventnor and the area covered by the Rural District Council grouped under South Wight council.

The Island's first stretch of dual carriageway, Medina Way, was opened at Newport from St Mary's Hospital to Coppins Bridge in 1975. The now notorious Coppins Bridge roundabout followed in 1984, but it was not until December, 1985, that the Newport south eastern relief road – from the roundabout to Shide – was completed.

Medina High School, at Fairlee, Newport, welcomed its first students in September, 1976. These were 285 13-year-olds. By 1982, after the completion of the building programme, the school had 1,306 on the roll, an indication of the school population bulge it was built to help cater for.

Medina's role as a dual-use community facility took on more definite shape when a theatre was opened on the campus in 1978, while September, 1980, saw the introduction of a £700,000 indoor heated swimming pool complex. This was in large measure due to the long and determined campaigning of the IW Indoor Swimming Pool Association, which although it had seen its dream of an Olympic-sized pool dashed at the eleventh hour in 1974 stuck to its task and contributed £35,000 to the joint-council-funded Medina pool.

Yarmouth lifeboat coxswain Dave Kennett was awarded the RNLI silver medal for gallantry in 1975 for the rescue of five London policemen in a Force 11 storm 14 miles south of the Needles. He later earned a bronze medal for another superb piece of seamanship when the lifeboat stood by a crippled ship off Swanage. Mr Kennett, who joined the Yarmouth crew in 1968, retired in 1994 after 23 years as coxswain and received the MBE in the Queen's Birthday honours a year later.

Yarmouth lifeboat coxswain Dave Kennett, MBE

The Island's three main councils aimed to hit the jackpot when they jointly launched a municipal lottery in 1978. It ran for eight years until falling sales forced its closure because it was no longer possible to keep running costs down to 25 percent of income as required by the gaming regulations. The net profit to Island ratepayers over the years from sales of approximately £1.5 million was around £400,000, with some £575,000 paid out in prizes, ranging from 25 pence to a £4,000 car.

A capsized West German tanker, the *Tarpenbek*, became an unlikely tourist attraction in Sandown Bay in June, 1979. The 999-ton vessel, carrying 1,500 gallons of oil, was damaged in a collision in fog off Selsey Bill with the Fleet Auxiliary vessel *Sir Geraint*. Although she survived the collision the *Tarpenbek* later rolled over after being battered by high winds. On the orders of the Department of Trade she was towed into Sandown Bay where a Dutch salvage crew, from the same company which had helped salvage the *Pacific Glory*, finally managed to pump out most of her cargo and right her so that she could be towed away.

To celebrate the successful conclusion of the month-long tricky operation Shanklin Hotel and Guest House Asssociation, which had initially sought an injunction to prevent the

The stricken tanker
Tarpenbek

Tarpenbek being brought into the bay because of the risk of pollution, organised a champagne and caviar party afloat for the salvage crews and others involved. Elaborate precautions had been taken to prevent beaches being polluted, including spraying any small slicks from the air with detergent. The pilot carrying out the spraying became known as Biggles and true to his fictional namesake he survived unscathed after his plane crashed into the sea and turned turtle.

1980 – 1990

The decade that marked the centenary of the *County Press* in November, 1984, also proved to be one of the most eventful in the history of the paper.

As previously noted, 1981 was a watershed in Island shopping patterns with the opening in the February of the county's first superstore, called Mainstop (later Somerfield) which was linked to International Stores, and the arrival in the July of Tesco's at Westridge, Ryde – the Island's first out of town superstore. A major leisure complex was built alongside, including an indoor swimming pool. Before the end of the '80s, Safeway had opened a large store in Church Litten, Newport, followed by one on the outskirts of Lake in February, 1992.

A giant bonfire on St Catherine's Down was literally a highlight of Island celebrations for the wedding of Prince Charles and Lady Diana Spencer in July, 1981.

During a December blizzard 55,000 Islanders, nearly half of the population, were temporarily without electricity in conditions described as the worst to hit the Island for 20 years. And in mid-January, 1982, the third blizzard in less than a month left snowdrifts up to seven feet deep blocking many roads, bringing traffic to a virtual halt and leading to school closures.

From a crisis at home to a much more serious one abroad: the Argentinian invasion of the Falklands saw many Islanders sailing with a task force to recapture the islands deep in the South Atlantic. Comprehensive *County Press* coverage brought home the agony of families and friends waiting for news of loved ones caught up in the brief but bloody four-month conflict.

In all but one case there was a happy ending, but for the family of 18-year-old sailor Andrew Swallow, of Bembridge, news that he had survived the *HMS Sheffield* disaster proved false. Instead, confirmation came that he was among the 20 men "dead or presumed dead" among the crew of the destroyer which caught fire and was abandoned after being hit by an Argentine missile.

Andrew's mother, Jill, was station director of IW Hospital Radio and it was her idea that Islanders with relatives or close friends serving with the Falklands task force should be given the opportunity to record messages to them through the station. Programme controller David Holbrook said: "This was purely Jill's idea and we are carrying it through because we all know this would be her wish."

With the return of the task force to Portsmouth, having successfully completed its mission to free the Falklands in two-and-a-half-months, the paper was soon full of joyful homecoming parties and reunions. These included soldier Graham Jervis, 19, of Greenways, Newport, who proposed to his girlfriend, Tania Sporne, 18, of Binstead Hill, Binstead, by telegram from the battle zone. Tania readily accepted and booked the date for the wedding.

The Island-built *Thrust Two* rocketed across the Black Rock Desert in the USA at an average speed of 633mph in 1983 to smash the world land speed record. There were six Islanders in the team, one of whom, John Ackroyd, of Ryde, designed the supercar. The same year a new era of cross-Solent car ferries made its bow when Sealink UK – now Wightlink – introduced the £4.5million *St Catherine* on the Portsmouth-Fishbourne route. She could carry 142 cars and 1,000 passengers, a massive increase on her predecessors.

Before the end of the year a sister ship, the *St Helen*, joined the *St Catherine* and two more, the *St Faith* and the *St Cecilia*, were to follow them later. There was an even more radical change on the Ryde-Portsmouth passenger ferry service in 1986 as two high-speed

Sealink's new fast catamaran *Our Lady Patricia*

catamarans, *Our Lady Patricia* and *Our Lady Pamela*, came into service, replacing the ageing motor vessels *Brading* and *Southsea*. Both vessels were named after the daughters of the late Earl Mountbatten of Burma. Remarkably, the 30-metre *Our Lady Pamela* made the voyage from her builders in Tasmania under her own power, completing the 14,000 miles in one-and-a-half-months.

In November, 1985, Lord Mottistone was appointed to succeed his half-brother, Sir John Nicholson, Bt., as the Island's Lord Lieutenant the following February. Lord Mottistone was the fourth son of that famous Islander, the first Baron Mottistone. Sir John had become Lord Lieutenant in 1980 in the wake of the murder of Earl Mountbatten, whom he had served as Vice-Lord Lieutenant.

Arctic conditions gripped the Island in January, 1985, as snow and a 19-day freeze-up led to 800 tons of salt and 1,000 tons of grit being used to try to keep traffic moving. County Hall was the nerve centre of an operation involving 220 men and 65 vehicles. Two years later there were similar scenes when another cold spell came. A *County Press* picture showed mini-icebergs in Wootton Creek.

Thousands of well-wishers turned out to greet Prince Andrew and his bride-to-be, Miss Sarah Ferguson, when the prince visited the Island for the Schneider Trophy Air Race in June, 1986.

Rarely can the truism that a picture can tell more than a thousand words have had greater relevance in the *County Press* than the photographs showing the trail of devastation left by the violent storm of hurricane force which hammered the Island in the early hours of Friday, October 16, 1987. A page of pictures showed timber decking and debris from Shanklin Pier piled on the beach after winds topping 100mph wrecked the 1,200ft long, 95-year-old structure; the Undercliff Drive completely blocked at St Lawrence; cars and homes caved in under fallen trees; and one of a number of caravans written off by other tree falls at a Freshwater holiday park.

Also pictured were the shattered remains of two greenhouses at Ralph's Garden Centre in Watergate Road, Newport, where three more were badly damaged and of firemen clearing trees from rooftops at Pound Mead Road, Ryde, before covering the gaping holes with tarpaulins. A total of 260 emergency calls were dealt with by the IW Fire and Rescue Service.

At the height of the storm some 200 roads were fully or partially closed by trees and debris and in some places, like Church Street, Ventnor, dangerous buildings made it necessary to close streets to traffic. The storm took a terrible toll of Ventnor Botanic Garden and Victoria Avenue, Shanklin, where 20 specimen trees straddled the road and garden walls. Again County Hall rose to the occasion, masterminding an operation that by the Saturday evening reduced the number of roads still blocked to less than 20.

 Although damage ran into millions of pounds, miraculously no-one was seriously injured though families had to be evacuated from a Medina Borough Council block of flats in Slade Road, Ryde, after the flat roof was blown off and at Newport a family of four scrambled to safety when the gables of their home in Medina Avenue collapsed and the roof was severely damaged.

In a sequel to the devastation the Countryside Management Service, with the aid of Government grants, launched an on-going replanting programme to replace the hundreds of trees smashed by a storm that no-one who experienced it will ever forget.

Newport Football Club celebrated its centenary year in 1988 by transferring from the club's Church Litten home, scene of some famous FA Cup encounters, to a £1.5 million new ground called St George's Park. The move was to make way for a new store development.

The same year Brading households became the first to have water meters installed after the Island was chosen as a guinea pig area to try out this system of charging for domestic supplies. In the event it did not result in the system being adopted nationally, at least not up to now.

Having officially opened the Earl Mountbatten Hospice at Fairlee, Newport, in October,

1982, the Duchess of Kent returned in November, 1988, to perform a similar ceremony for the new cancer day care centre attached to the hospice. Like the first, this second project was the result of a major public fund-raising effort, with Islanders again showing their remarkable generosity by contributing £325,000 in 16 months — £35,000 more than the original target.

With Shanklin Pier finished off by the hurricane, misfortune struck Sandown Pier in August, 1989, when fire severely damaged an amusement arcade and dressing rooms at the Pavilion theatre. Seventy firemen fought the blaze and managed to prevent the theatre being destroyed. (Jimmy Tarbuck's *Summer Magic Show*, made homeless by the fire, was quickly back on stage at Shanklin Theatre). After work costing £2 million, the complex was re-opened the following June by owner Mr George Peak, who pumped in £600,000 of his own money on top of the £1.4 million insurance pay-out to restore and improve the pier.

After a hot, dry summer, Southern Water was crying out for water to replenish supplies. The company's prayers were partly answered in December as torrential rain brought flooding to many parts of the Island. But the storms also caused considerable damage, with sea defences at Seaview, St Helens and Gurnard bearing the brunt.

1990 – 2000

The '90s produced yet another example of the bond between the *County Press* and the community it serves. Never is that tie closer than in times of adversity and the Gulf War, triggered by the Iraqi invasion of Kuwait, saw the paper instantly reacting to the anxiety of the situation as more than 150 Island servicemen and women were sent to the war zone. Each week through the crisis provoked by Iraqi dictator Saddam Hussein, the paper played its part in bringing relatives and friends closer to their loved ones taking part in Operation Desert Storm, which began in January, 1991.

Several Islanders working in Kuwait or Iraq were taken hostage and after reporting on their harrowing ordeal, the paper told of the relief at their release and safe return home. Through articles, photographs and messages a special feature at Christmas, 1990, let those from the Island serving in the Gulf and those they had left behind show how much they cared. The feature also made sure that servicemen and women facing dangers in Northern Ireland were not forgotten.

The activities of the Gulf Island Families Together were widely reported. This support group sent out hundreds of food and gift parcels and also had its own hotline manned by volunteers offering support and advice for relatives and friends. There were a number of casualties among Island servicemen but no deaths were reported. The routing of Iraqi forces by the end of February, 1991, brought immense relief all-round and meant the paper could concentrate on the joy of homecomings.

Award-winning Island-born actor Jeremy Irons helped to launch the Island's own radio station on Easter Sunday, 1990 – the sequel to years of campaigning led by Mr Pat Norris, of Cowes, and a triumph for the young joint managing directors, Jean Paul Hansford and Steve Oates.

Cowes Express livened up the cross-Solent scene by launching a fast ferry service between

Cowes and Southampton in May, 1990, but after a turbulent couple of years the company was wound up.

Having been taken over by Associated British Ports about 18 months before, Red Funnel made a major new impact on its Cowes to Southampton passenger service by launching two catamaran-style, twin-hulled fast ferries in 1991. *Red Jet I* and *II*, built by FBM at Cowes, represented a £3.5 million investment to phase out hydrofoils that had been in service on the route since 1969. *Red Jet III* came on line in July, 1998.

In April, 1996, the arrival on the East Cowes to Southampton service of Red Funnel's £8 million flagship *Red Eagle* completed an investment of some £25 million in new car ferry tonnage. Also on the ferry scene, Wightlink was sold by Sea Containers to Cinven, one of Europe's leading venture capital groups, in June, 1995, in a £107 million deal. American-controlled Sea Containers had bought the whole of the 36-strong Sealink fleet 11 years earlier for £66 million.

Princess Alexandra, in September, 1991, officially opened the £29 million St Mary's Hospital at Newport, hailed as a pioneering energy-saving building. But the Island's new district hospital had been two years late in receiving its first patients the previous April and in fact came into use four years late compared with the original timetable. Despite its marvellous modern facilities, St Mary's was on the sick list by 1995 as rust problems began to emerge with the steel cladding that had been a controversial feature of the building from the outset. The ultimate outcome was a £26 million repair and improvement programme for what at the opening had been described as a "world class hospital".

The 1993 New Year's Honours included the OBE for Mr Roy Harris, of Whitwell, in recognition of the way he masterminded the raising of £500,000 to buy the Island's own bodyscanner, a magnificent achievement which was to prove the forerunner a few years later of the *County Press* sponsored MRI scanner appeal..

August that year saw the *County Press* in the news as it recruited a star name to its editorial team – paving the way for valuable free publicity for the Island in the process. Michael Palin, the actor and writer famed for his hugely successful TV series, *Around the World in 80 Days* and *Pole to Pole*, became a guest columnist. His assignment was to write four monthly columns on aspects of Island life in his own inimitable style, which in turn was the focal point of a documentary series for Meridian TV, called *Palin's Column*, which was nationally networked later.

Michael Palin, a new, if temporary, recruit to the *County Press* editorial team in 1993

The continuing saga of a proposed fixed link with the mainland entered a new chapter as Winchester-based Linkland Ltd unveiled its initial blueprint for a £30 million tunnel from Ryde seafront to Gillkicker Point, west of Gosport. Traffic would take turns in crossing one way at a time. The *County Press* tested public opinion on the issue. A record-breaking phone-in poll for a weekly paper, with nearly 7,000 responding, came out more than two-to-one against the idea of a fixed link – 4,818 to 2,027.

The subject was to re-emerge in 1998 when the findings of a £100.000 study concluded that such a link could be viable but was unlikely to be cheaper than off-peak ferry fares at a suggested £15 each way toll for a car. The 143-page feasibility study came out in favour of an immersed tunnel, costing around £230 million, including infrastructure.

Four engineers at Westland Aerospace, East Cowes, scooped a near £300,000 pools jackpot with Littlewoods but despite massive orders in the pipeline their employers were experiencing a tough time. The company announced a further 264 redundancies, bringing job losses to almost 550 in two years.

The headline over the review of the year, "When man and nature wreaked havoc on IW" summed up 1994. The man-made havoc was the firebomb blitz that wrecked much of the Boots store at Newport; burned out the interior of the Sports and Model Shop in Union Street, Ryde; caused serious smoke damage to the next door Coffee Shop snack bar and gutted the Ryde Cancer Research Shop. Damage was estimated at £3 million.

The graphic editorial and pictorial coverage of this outrage saw *County Press* sales top 40,000 copies in a week for the first time.

The massive investigation into the incident was a classic of painstaking and determined police work which, in 1997, led to animal rights activist Barry Horne, 45, of Birmingham, being convicted of the offences. He was sentenced to 18 years imprisonment for the Island attacks and offences at Bristol.

On the weather front, torrential rain in January, 1994, turned some streets into rivers and subsidence-prone areas into sponges. A huge landslide at Blackgang left two houses in ruins and a 60ft section of Old Blackgang Road leading from the Chine to Southview Holiday Park collapsed down the cliff on to the beach.

The long-running issue of if and when Marks and Spencer would come to the Island had a positive conclusion in March, 1994, with the opening of a £14 million store next to Safeway at Newport. Two years later BHS gave further emphasis to Newport's reputation as the Island's shopping mecca by opening a store in High Street, while April, 1999, saw Sainsbury's

The aftermath of the firebombing of Boots store in Newport High Street

making its debut on the Island at Hunnyhill.

An audacious escape by three dangerous prisoners from Parkhurst Prison in January, 1995, was to have far-reaching repercussions as it became the latest chapter in a national jail crisis. The escape, involving the use of a master key, was not discovered until the three were reported missing from a PE session. Extensive media coverage and a political outcry led to the immediate removal from his job of the Parkhurst governor, the late John Marriott, whom many saw as a scapegoat.

A chance sighting by an off-duty prison officer led to the trio's recapture in the Binfield area five days after they went on the run, having apparently failed in an initial attempt to take an aircraft from the IW Airport at Sandown. The breakout led to Parkhurst losing its Category A status, a downgrading resulting in the loss of 100 jobs among officers and civilian staff.

The area between Luccombe and Bonchurch, appropriately known as The Landslip, lived up to its name in February, 1995, as an estimated 1.5 million tonnes of earth subsided.

Two months later a milestone in local government was marked as the Island became the first area in the country to have a new-style unitary authority. The county council was renamed the IW Council as it also took over the responsibilities from Medina and South Wight borough councils. The streamlining saw the shedding of some 400 jobs.

October provided a creepy crawly sequel to the long hot summer when Bembridge CE Primary School was temporarily closed by an infestation of poisonous Spanish spiders. The insects are native to the Canary Islands and are known to have reached the South Coast of England in the last ten years.

Showing that the Island can compete with the best, The Wight Mouse Inn at Chale was named UK Family Pub of the Year in the *Good Pub Guide*, having scooped a similar accolade earlier in the year – more were to follow.

As 1995 came to a close Lord Mottistone was succeeded as the Island's Lord Lieutenant by Mr Christopher Bland, managing director of Hovertravel.

Early the following year Island farmers warned that unless the EU rescinded a ban on imported British beef arising from the BSE crisis, many local beef and dairy farmers would face bankruptcy and farm closures. But there was a fillip for the Island tourist industry as the Seaview Hotel at Seaview came top in a Department of National Heritage survey of small hotels throughout the country – and other plaudits lay in store for the Seaview Hotel as the decade progressed.

Bruce Goldsmith, 35, of Newport, and Innes Powell, 31, of Ryde, became the first pilots to paraglide from the Island to the mainland.

The CP played Cupid to a couple, of whom the bride-to-be reached the final of a national bridal competition. Sarah McCullum, 26, deputy bar manager at Warner's Bembridge holiday centre, and L/Cpl Mark Arden got together after the paper published an appeal from an army mother requesting pen-friends for soldiers serving in Bosnia.

It was like a film script come true when Anthony Minghella became the local boy to make very good, winning the Oscar for Best Director in March, 1997, for his film *The English Patient* – one of nine awarded to the film. A jubilant Anthony, who also wrote the script, made special mention of his Isle of Wight birthplace before a television audience of millions around the world as he picked up one of the film world's most coveted accolades at the Hollywood ceremony.

The honours won by *The English Patient* – the best-ever tally by a British film – were all the more remarkable because at one stage it was in danger of not being made when backers, 20th Century Fox, pulled out just two days before shooting was due to start. Such was the faith of the cast, that they stayed on location in Italy while Anthony and producer Saul Zaentz flew back to America and convinced Miramax Films to back them.

Anthony's proud parents, Eddie and Gloria Minghella, of Spencer Road, Ryde, who appeared as extras in the film, saw to it that it was not only international publicity which the Island gained from their son's success. The day after the British premiere in London there was a gala screening of the film at Newport's Medina Movie Theatre, which raised £10,000 for the MRI scanner appeal. The pride Islanders took in Anthony's achievements showed itself when he was made the first Honorary Freeman of the Island. The following day, when he waved his Oscar aloft while posing for a *County Press* picture in his home town, shoppers broke into spontaneous applause and shouted their congratulations.

One of the most heart-rending stories ever to appear in the *County Press* had a sad ending in early December, 1997, with the death of courageous mother Anita Mead, 33, of Sandown. Anita had captured hearts across the world with her decision to sacrifice her own future to have a child. Since telling in February, 1997, how she had earlier refused treatment for cervical cancer so the life of her then unborn daughter, Hannah, could be protected, Anita's plight had captured global attention.

Her mother, Mrs Rose Rapley, said the interest aroused by the *County Press* story had given Anita renewed hope and extended her life. Anita's greatest dream came true in June when she married David, 48, the man she called the rock in her valiant but eventually unsuccessfuly battle against cancer.

The night sky of the Island was lit by beacons in March, 1998, on the eve of the national Countryside March which saw 700 Islanders travel to London for a massive protest in defence of Britain's traditional rural way of life. Brilliant columnist Charlotte Hofton was part of the CP editorial team which covered the event.

A dream round-the-world cruise almost ended in tragedy for Peter and Doreen Cheek, of Wootton. They had to swim for their lives after their yacht was wrecked in heavy seas on Maatsuker Island, south of Tasmania. It was their second narrow escape – they survived the storm that cost 17 lives in the 1979 Fasnet Race from Cowes. There was a fairy tale ending for the Cheeks as the kind folk of Tasmania and relatives and friends on the Island responded to their plight with gifts in kind and cash. Their 42ft yacht sloop *Talis II* was salvaged and after carrying out repairs the Cheeks set sail on a shake-down cruise to New Zealand in May, 1999 – a year after their circumnavigation was so dramatically interrupted.

Having scored a major triumph at the first elections for the new IW Council three years before, Liberal Democrats took a severe mauling the second time round, but despite having their representation cut from 31 seats to 16 they just managed to cling to power. The Tories, with 15 seats, staged a big comeback but it was Independents and Labour members who had the deciding say over who would run the authority.

After a series of protests and delays work finally started on Southern Water's £100 million

Seaclean Wight scheme to pump most of the Island's sewage out to sea at Yaverland in Sandown Bay via a 3km outfall. The company had faced tremendous opposition to its plans, particularly over the standard of treatment that waste would receive before it entered the outfall. There was a breakthrough when deputy prime minister John Prescott included the Island scheme as one of six along the South Coast which must now incorporate secondary treatment into the disposal process. The outcome is that initially primary treatment equipment is being installed with secondary treatment following on.

What looked like the final chapter in the long-running saga of the St Mary's Hospital Koan was written at the end of July. Hospital chiefs decided that the hugely controversial £55,000 sculpture should remain on its site outside the hospital – illuminated at night but not revolving as originally intended. They described themselves as in a "no win" situation because if they ordered the removal of the 26ft high structure the cost of repaying grants would come from funds for patient care, unlike the money used to buy the Koan.

The Island's own television station, TV 12, was officially launched at the end of October, 1998, with an experienced American, Paul Meade, as managing director. The new terrestrial channel had hoped to start sooner in the year but was delayed until French broadcasters made certain it would not interfere with their stations.

Cowes had an early Christmas present with the news that Cowes Week was to be supported by Skandia Life into the new millennium with a £1 million-plus sponsorship deal.

Islanders' reputation for supporting good causes found fresh expression when more than 1,000 items were donated to the CP-sponsored Christmas toy appeal. Social Services arranged for 120 disadvantaged Island children to receive a sackful of toys and games each. There were still plenty left over and these were sent to needy children in Romania and Chernobyl.

With its long and distinguished career as a theatre having ended the previous September – the victim of falling audiences – the former Sandown Pavilion began a new lease of life just before Easter, 1999, as a multi-use, all-year-round entertainment complex. The auditorium was transformed into an Amazon-style jungle scene setting for crazy golf, with ten pin bowling also on offer and the former balcony given over to a children's adventure play area.

The prospect of the biggest boost in recent years for the Island's economy came with the news that a rapidly expanding manufacturing company was to set up here and create 250 jobs. Danish-owned Aerolaminates announced plans to build a £13 million flagship headquarters at St Cross Business Park at Newport, for the manufacture of wood composite wind turbine blades.

More welcome news on the employment front was generated by self-made millionaire Bob Potter, whose Lakeside complex at Frimley Green, Surrey, is the Mecca for world darts. He revealed plans for a hotel and conference and exhibition centre on a 16-acre site behind the Westridge Leisure Centre, at Ryde, creating up to 140 new jobs.

Hundred of spectators watched in horror as a plane crashed at Bembridge Airport, killing its pilot instantly. Mainlander David Milne, 33, died when his Cassut racing aircraft fell to the ground about 100 metres from the Propeller Inn, as he was trying to qualify for a race being held as part of the Schneider Trophy event

As this book approached completion, the *County Press* was publicising a campaign for the Island to retain its distinctive and coveted DL vehicle number plate. Chief sub-editor Alan Marriott coined the headline What DL is going on? for a report that many Islanders were opposed to a Government proposal to do away with the DL registration, replacing it with an H for Hampshire as part of a nationwide restructuring of the registration system. A petition declared: "The Island is determined that it will not be forgotten or seen as part of Hampshire. The DL registration is symbolic of the IW's uniqueness and its determination to remain visibly separated from mainland England."

Bearing in mind that one of the main issues the *County Press* pursued when it was first published was the campaign for the Island to win local authority independence from Hampshire, this was clearly a case of history repeating itself as the paper and its readers united in an independence fight with a difference. ◆